ST. AUGUSTINE'S BONES

ST. AUGUSTINE'S BONES

A Microhistory

HAROLD SAMUEL STONE

University of Massachusetts Press
AMHERST AND BOSTON

Printed in the United States of America

LC 2002069568
ISBN 1-55849-387-5 (cloth); 388-3 (paper)

Designed by Dean Bornstein
Set in Adobe Caslon with Golden Cockerel display by Graphic Composition, Inc.
Printed and bound by Sheridan Books, Inc.

Library of Congress Cataloging-in-Publication Data

Stone, Harold Samuel, 1949–
St. Augustine's bones : a microhistory / Harold Samuel Stone.
p. cm. — (Studies in print culture and the history of the book)
Includes bibliographical references and index.
ISBN 1-55849-387-5 (alk. paper) — ISBN 1-55849-388-3 (pbk. : alk. paper)
1. Augustine, Saint, Bishop of Hippo—Relics—Italy—Pavia—History—17th century. I. Title. II. Series.

BR1720.A9 S86 2002
235'.2—dc21

2002069568

British Library Cataloguing in Publication data are available.

This book is published with the support of The Gladys Krieble Delmas Foundation.

For Melissa, Emily, and Edward

CONTENTS

ACKNOWLEDGMENTS

My interest in the curious history of St. Augustine's relics began when, thinking I was on the way to somewhere else, I came across a collection of manuscripts and pamphlets in the Marciana Library in Venice that concerned a controversy about the saint's remains. The research for the project that grew out of this chance encounter was supported by many institutions and encouraged by many friends. The Gladys Krieble Delmas Foundation made possible the preliminary research. Colgate University provided support and awarded me a Paul Garrison fellowship. The American University in Cairo offered generous grants that permitted several research trips to Pavia and to academic libraries in the United States.

I have relied on the expertise and assistance of many librarians. Much of the primary research was conducted at the Biblioteca Universitaria di Pavia; I am especially grateful for the help I received from the staff of the rare books and manuscript section there. I also appreciated the graciousness of the librarians during my visits to the Biblioteca di San Pietro in Ciel d'Oro in Pavia. It was a pleasure to be able to use the newly renovated Biblioteca Ambrosiana and the Braidense in Milan. Significant portions of this research were carried out at the Marciana in Venice, the British Library in London, and the libraries of the universities of Pittsburgh, of Pennsylvania, and of Texas, and at Indiana University. The interlibrary loan staffs at Pittsburgh and Indiana were of immense assistance in obtaining books and articles, and the University of Pittsburgh Department of History granted me adjunct status which allowed me to use their libraries.

My work on St. Augustine benefited greatly from an NEH Summer Seminar for College Teachers, "Augustine and his Influence", directed by Jim O'Donnell. The seminar, conducted at Bryn Mawr, gave me access to the college's research collections, as well as those of the University of Pennsylvania, the Augustinian Institute, and Villanova. Jim O'Donnell has been a great help in bringing this project to fruition, and my primary thanks go to him. Parts of the manuscript were the basis for papers I delivered at meetings of the American Society for Eighteenth-Century

Studies, the Society for the History of Authorship, Reading, and Publishing, and the History of the Book Seminar at Indiana University. Allen Fitzgerald of the Augustinian Institute at Villanova University provided generous assistance.

This book is a microhistory. While part of the story concerns the experiences of ordinary people, a significant portion is about ordinary scholars, that is, individuals who are all but forgotten. This book is premised on the conviction that a people's religious experience cannot be separated from their cultural context. Knowing this as an abstract principle was not the same as putting it into practice in a historical narrative. Conversations about this issue have shaped my approach to this topic. In the course of my research I became convinced that the methods developed for the study of the history of the book, of reading, and of literacy were particularly suited to describe the controversy that arose in Pavia concerning the authenticity of St. Augustine's bones. I also learned a good deal from chats with Tia Kolbaba about formal religion and the ways it sometimes conflicted with the religious experience of believers in medieval Byzantium. Jim Toth and Ginny Danielson helped me understand the function of saints, of holy men and women, and their place in the urban traditions of contemporary Cairo. Jim O'Donnell offered useful suggestions on how to present the arguments about the bones and their significance. I benefited from conversations with Walter Lammi and with Max Grober on how to teach theological, scientific, and philosophic concerns in the historical context of the Enlightenment. Two peer review readers for the University of Massachusetts Press provided useful suggestions on earlier drafts of the manuscript. Paul Wright, editor at the University of Massachusetts Press, gave useful advice and a great deal of encouragement. Carol Betsch, managing editor, and the press staff turned the manuscript into a pleasing volume. The delicate copyediting of Amanda Heller touched and brought clarity to every page. Rebecca Ammerman and Albert Ammerman, friends whom I met at Colgate University, have helped me in a variety of ways to finish this book.

H. S. S.

ST. AUGUSTINE'S BONES

ONE
The Discovery of St. Augustine's Bones

ON Tuesday morning, October 1, 1695, a group of masons, a painter, and a sculptor arrived at the crypt of the Cathedral of San Pietro in Ciel d'Oro (St. Peter in the Golden Heaven) in the city of Pavia to do some repair work. Pavia, a university town of the province of Lombardy, is located some thirty-five kilometers to the southwest of Milan on the old road to Genoa. In 1695, Pavia was ruled by the Spanish, whose administrative seat was in Milan. Spain was at war with France: this has been called the War of the League of Augsburg, or the Nine Years' War, and in histories of the colonial period of the United States, it is known as King William's War. This time Pavia had escaped much of the horror of early modern warfare—except, of course, higher taxes. Though we cannot be certain, that October day had probably begun with one of Pavia's splendid fogs, whose mists occlude the stark brick towers that were the characteristic feature of the city's skyline (a number still exist). It was a rainy time of year, which meant it was dark in the church and the men needed torchlight to do their work. Their primary task was to install little decorative brackets or consoles on the crypt altar. Distinctive features of the crypt area were its columns of black marble and its two separate staircases, one reserved for the Augustinian Hermits and the other for the Canons Regular, the two orders sharing the church.

The foreman of the crew was Giovanni Battista Polino; Giacomo Rossi, Giuseppe Noveroni, Giacomo Torrioni, and Andrea Bonello, who were masons and stonecutters by profession, assisted him. Giuseppe Salo, who had fashioned the new altar ornament, was there with his son Francesco. Salo was from Milan, but had lived in Pavia for the past eleven years. The thirty-year-old painter Marco Antonio Pellino was present, and so was another painter, Tomaso Gatto, age fifty-five. Assessing the situation, Rossi judged that some rebuilding of the rear of the altar might be needed. The men couldn't begin their work until a low wall or barrier on the back of the altar had been removed, and they would have to pull up at least four of the paving stones on the floor behind the altar. Someone went to find the sacristan, Castelli, for the Augustinian Hermits. After listening to their plan, he gave them permission to proceed. The masons got to work, and Giuseppe Salo took a hammer and began breaking down the wall or protrusion behind the altar. They then raised the paving stones. As they began to clear away the debris and clutter, someone noticed a piece of white rock. The stonecutters immediately identified it as Carrara marble. More careful digging made it clear that they had come upon some sort of marble box, later determined to measure about four feet by one foot by one.[1]

The men stopped working, deciding to proceed only in the presence of the sacristan. Anyway, it was time for a break, so they had lunch. (Some later remembered eating lunch after the box had been removed but not yet opened.) With two torches for illumination, they then went back to take out the box. Pellino, the painter, who was looking down from above as the others extracted the box, saw some letters written in charcoal on the top. He could make out clearly *AU, O,* and *T.* He shouted out, "It's St. Augustine, it's St. Augustine!"; everyone then joined him in calling out the saint's name. The sculptor Giuseppe Salo later recalled seeing the whole name, spelled "Agostino," written out in capital letters; it was handwritten, not engraved, and he was certain that the style of the writing was exactly the way "we write Italian." Others reported that they had read "Augustino" and spoke of "Gothic lettering."[2] Salo's son Francesco, who couldn't read but knew his letters, could see clearly that there was an *A,* a *V,* an *S,* and an *O.* Giuseppe Rossi, who couldn't read but also knew his letters, supported what others had seen.[3] According to some recollections the name was writ-

1. Cleonice Baggini measured the marble box and the silver box it contained for his 1913 doctoral dissertation. The marble box was 187 cm. by 64 by 94; the silver box was 70 cm. by 37 by 24. Cleonice Baggini, "Storia della polemica intorno all'identità delle ossa di S. Agostino, vescovo e dottore della Chiesa, scoperte l'anno 1695 nella Basilica di S. Pietro in Ciel d'Oro di Pavia," Ph.D. diss. (Regia University, Pavia, 1913), 30, 31.

2. On the general issues of Latin and Italian writing and the use of different scripts, see A. Petrucci, "La scrittura tra ideologia e rappresentazione," in *Storia dell'arte italiana* (Turin: Einaudi, 1980), 9:5–123.

3. Michele Colli, *Responsio novis motivis fisci cum productione omnium jurium spectantium ad identitatem vener. ossium S. Augustini noviter inventorum* (February 17, 1699); reprinted in Fulgenzio Bellelli, *Collectio actorum atque allegatorum quibus ossa sacra Ticini in confessione S.P.C. et anno 1695 reperta esse S. Augustini Hipp. Episopi et Ecclesiae Doctoris,* 2 vols. (Venice: Sebastiano Coleti, 1729), 1:65–76. There is no mention in these testimonies of Gothic script.

ten on both the bottom and the top of the box. From subsequent questioning it became clear that while not all the workmen claimed to read Italian, they all knew their letters, and a number believed they could distinguish Italian from Latin.[4] That is, they were aware that there were different kinds of scripts, and some claimed an ability to distinguish between them.[5] Everyone agreed that no designation of saint, "Sanctus" or "Santo," appeared on the box.[6]

Having removed the box, they saw that it was closed by a little clasp, and that the corners were reinforced with lead. In forcing the clasp they did some damage to the marble box. Inside it they found a carved marble box; it contained a silver box decorated with simple crosses—Lombard crosses. This box was also locked, and they broke this clasp as well. A third box made of lead was mentioned in some accounts of the event. No such box exists. The confusion about it comes from the descriptions of the silver box by the some of the workmen who misidentified it as tin or lead. As they opened it they found a cloth veil, a lower jawbone with teeth, parts of a skull, numerous other bones, some glass vials, and a lot of blackish dust. At this point they realized that they should go no further. A proper exhumation needed to be made so they packed everything away more or

---

The claim of Gothic lettering was accepted by both sides of the ensuing controversy. It was part of the oral tradition that developed around the invention. After Crippa's death it was asserted that he had seen the writing; no official statement was made by him on this matter.

4. Carlo M. Cipolla, *Literacy and Development in the West* (Baltimore: Penguin Books, 1969), 57, cites a payroll document of the Fabbrica del Duomo in Milan for 1586–95, in which 52 of 104 workers signed their names. Of these men, 10 were sculptors, 9 of whom could write their name. These Pavian workers followed the same trades and were from similar social classes as their Milanese predecessors. Being able to read letters is not the same skill as knowing how to write one's name. And we do not know how, when, or even if Francesco's father planned on passing on his literacy skills to his son. See also Peter Burke, "The Uses of Literacy in Early Modern Italy," in *The Social History of Language,* ed. Peter Burke and Roy Porter (Cambridge: Cambridge University Press, 1987), 21–42.

5. This is an example of what William Harris calls "craftsman's literacy" in early modern times, e.g., in *Ancient Literacy* (Cambridge: Harvard University Press, 1989), 7–8. Harvey J. Graff, *The Legacies of Literacy* (Bloomington: Indiana University Press, 1987), 21, uses the term "craft literacy." Brian Street speaks of "Maktab literacy" to describe a similar level of literacy in an Iranian village of the 1970s which has certain parallels to the case of Pavia. See also Brian Street, *Literacy in Theory and Practice* (Cambridge: Cambridge University Press, 1984), 153, and more generally chap. 5.

6. Bellelli, *Collectio actorum* (1729), 1:49–59.

less as they had found it. Unfortunately, the abbot of the Canons Regular, the other Augustinian order sharing the cathedral with the Hermits, was out of town. An assemblage of the principals could not be scheduled until five days later.

For the men involved, this event brought them into contact with what they regarded as the sacred. This was something different from the annual cycle of celebrations which honored a local patron saint. In discovering the relics, which they believed to be those of St. Augustine, they had entered into his myth, the sacred story of the patron saint of Pavia. The act of finding lost or forgotten relics was part of the Catholic experience of sainthood, though to be actually involved in such a discovery was rare. The technical term for it was "Invention." The role of these workers was no longer that of a passive listener to the stories told about the saint. What they had previously known as the timeless tale of their patron saint had suddenly become part of their own personal time and place. This experience of finding the saint's body thus had a heightened immediacy, though in principle it was no different from the spiritual aim of the Catholic Mass or of believers' interaction with the divine through prayer. The men who found the body, and the community that responded with enthusiasm to its discovery, were involved in a spiritual experience outside their day-to-day existence. This chance event brought them into direct contact with one of the defining elements of their community, its patron saint. Tradition made clear what should happen next that would reaffirm this patron-client relationship: miracles would occur, and the spiritual life around San Pietro would be enriched. And once the discovery had received official sanction, the community's spiritual leaders were expected to inform the laity through printed essays and perhaps sermons about the meaning and significance of this experience. Religious officials in Pavia recognized that there were different communities of readers and auditors—what Stanley Fish calls "interpretive communities"—who would encounter these written materials and oral reports in a variety of forms and formats. These individuals, in their silent reading and in their conversation, constituted one of those little groups whose involvement with the printed word marked the beginnings of a general reading public.[7] An aim of this book is to show

7. Stanley Fish, *Is There a Text in This Class? The Authority of Interpretive Communities* (Cambridge: Harvard University Press, 1980). See also Roger Chartier, "Communities of Readers," in *The Order of Books: Readers, Authors, and Libraries in Europe between the Fourteenth and Eighteenth Centuries,* trans. Lydia G. Cochrane (Cambridge: Polity Press, 1992),

how this audience of listeners and readers, who for the most part left no written response to what they read or were told, interacted and influenced the interpretation of this event.

The bones were discovered at a time when Catholic religious scholars were in disagreement as to the significance of relics for Catholic spirituality and in the emphasis they should receive in local parish life. It was argued that a thorough historical investigation of such relics was needed to verify their authenticity.[8] Some questioned whether all of the nameless skeletons found in the Roman catacombs, a traditional source for relics, could be considered martyrs to Christ. A few argued that a variety of interpretations might be ascribed to specific relics, and did not insist on an uncontroversial, straightforward yes-or-no answer on their authenticity. They believed that probability and tradition should be allowed a degree of moral suasion in such cases. Some even took the position that an indeterminacy of meaning, properly understood within the context of the available historical evidence, could be more edifying to a believer than either the dogmatic acceptance of any single tradition or the skeptical rejection of all of them. Their aim was to support the religious enthusiasm generated for relics with a spirit of moderation founded on sound historical investigation. Authentic spirituality, they argued, was communal, individualized, and even private, while religion had a public aspect; the true believer lived as a responsible person, respectful of the opinions of others.

Subtle consideration of evidence, however, had no place in the initial investigation carried out in Pavia. After Vespers in the early evening of Saturday, October 5, Tomaso Antonio Scotto, a representative of the papacy, Lorenzo Trotta, bishop of Pavia, Carlo Bernardino Trovato, the abbot of the Canons Regular, Giuseppe Crippa, the abbot of the Augustinian Hermits, the notary Pietro Nabona, and other witnesses gathered at the crypt altar of San Pietro's. Their primary purpose was to find anything that would provide a positive identification of the bones or relics. They were told how the master stonecutters had opened the boxes. Nothing was found on either the exterior or the interior of the various boxes that gave any hint to the identity of the relics. No trace—certainly nothing legible—

1–23; Robert Darnton, "First Steps toward a History of Reading," in *The Kiss of Lamourette: Reflections in Cultural History* (New York: W. W. Norton, 1990), 154–87.

8. Girolamo Imbruglia, "Dalle storie di santi alla storia naturale della religione: l'idea moderna di superstizione," *Rivista storica Italiana*, 101 (1989), 35–84.

was left of the charcoal writing that had fired the imagination of the workmen. Perhaps it had been rubbed off when the casket was replaced or when it was opened the first time. The officials made no hypothesis of identity or the provenance of the bones; it was determined, however, to have an inventory of the bones prepared by expert anatomists. The boxes were returned to the altar under lock and key, and guards from both orders, the Hermits and the Canons Regular, continued the watch they had begun on the first of October. There were four locks and keys, two assigned to each order.

Representatives of both orders conducted a series of interviews with the workers between November 1695 and February 1696; a similar examination was held in February and March of 1698.[9] On February 9, 1696, two renowned anatomists, Carlo Gualla and Domenico Bernardi, completed the first of several enumerations of the bones. A second list was prepared in the middle of March by Gualla and Giovanni Maria Bonelli. The locations of other relics of Augustine were compiled. Augustine's heart was in a reliquary in Antwerp; it was said to vibrate when the word "Trinity" was spoken. To remove the heart, his body must have been cut up, and hence, it was asserted, the fragmentary condition of the bones was not surprising. There was an earnestness in the proceedings, a seriousness of purpose, and an enthusiasm about the discovery; yet at the same time, the documents suggest that other forces blocked prompt recognition of the authenticity of the relics. Only in February 1698 was Michele Colli, a Franciscan, or to be more exact a Barnabite, appointed to prepare the case concerning the relics found in San Pietro. He was an elderly man who had served as an official on the bishop of Pavia's Inquisitorial Court. On the thirteenth and the fifteenth of March, the leaders of the two orders, the papal representative, and the archbishop again gathered to review the evidence but made no new determination. By that time several miracles had occurred, all attributed to the newfound relics. The belief in the authenticity of the relics had progressed far faster than the ecclesiastical authority's ability to verify with certainty that these were indeed St. Augustine's bones.

The news of the discovery had spread around Catholic Italy. By the

9. Early examples of recollections about written evidence can be found in Michael T. Clanchy, *From Memory to Written Record: England, 1066–1307* (Cambridge: Harvard University Press, 1979), 175–77.

middle of October 1695, it was being discussed with enthusiastic amazement in Naples.[10] In early November, Ludovico Muratori, at this time a young man yet to make his international reputation, wanting more news about the relics, wrote to Antonio Magliabecchi, the librarian of the Grand Duke of Tuscany, who had a reputation as a bottomless pit of erudition and intellectual gossip. They exchanged what information was known, and in early January 1696, Muratori noted that all the hubbub seemed to have vanished because of the lack of evidence.[11] Muratori had just moved from Modena to Milan in February 1695; it is indicative of how local events of this sort were that it made sense for Muratori to write to Florence to clarify what was going on in Pavia just thirty miles away.

Finding the bones of a saint was an unusual event. The most common discoveries in sacred buildings were of old images, often frescoes that had been forgotten or concealed by previous renovations and repairs. It was not uncommon for the discovery of these images to be accompanied by miraculous cures and even visions. The officials of the Catholic Church assigned in the seventeenth and eighteenth centuries to investigate the authenticity of such visions and cures seldom pronounced the objects to be worthy of veneration or the cures to be miracles. Finding relics in a sacred space was another matter.[12] Still, the circumstances of the find in Pavia were unspectacular in comparison to other near-contemporary discoveries of saintly corpses. For example, in 1648, when the tomb of Pope Sylvester II was opened in Rome, the body, buried in the eleventh century, was found to be intact and to produce sweet odors. This was important for Sylvester's reputation, for the traditions about him were not flattering. He was the first French pope, and according to some a magician whose rapid advancement

10. Domenico Confuorto, *Giornale di Napoli dal MDCLXXXIX al MDCIC,* ed. Nicola Nicolini (Naples: Lubrano, 1930), 2:185. Confuorto, who was probably a notary or a lawyer, managed to pick up a good deal of information. Not only did he know about the finding of the body, but also his information source must have mentioned the two Translations of Augustine's body and that the relics had been lost for many years.

11. Ludovico Muratori, *Epistolario,* ed. Matteo Campori (Modena: Società Tipografia Modenese, 1901) 1:107 (no. 85), 115 (no. 89), and 125 (no. 99).

12. The discovery of the relics of Saints Aymo and Vermondis, the founders of Milan's S. Vittore in Meda, is a case in point. The Invention of the relics was in 1619, the ceremony of their Translation to a new shrine in 1626. An account of the event was published in 1629 and again in 1741. Robert Kendrick, *Celestial Sirens: Nuns and Their Music in Early Modern Milan* (Oxford: Clarendon Press, 1996), 163–64, 449. Kendrick ranks the music and the ceremony as among the most magnificent in early-seventeenth-century Milan.

was the result of a pact made with hell; his career had culminated, some said, when the devil snatched him away. Another example occurred in England in 1685 during the coronation of James II at Westminster. The scaffolding erected for the ceremony seems to have damaged the wooden coffin of Edward the Confessor. A curious chorister, along with some friends, decided to investigate. They found numerous bones, a skull with all the teeth intact, and a golden crucifix and chain. James subsequently reinterred the bones with great pomp.[13] Another case occurred in 1698 at Benevento's main cathedral, where the bones of the apostle Bartholemew were found; his flayed skin was in Rome, preserved because he had been a tanner by trade, and memorialized in Michelangelo's fresco *The Last Judgment.*

Although the official inquest of October 1695 reached no conclusion on the identity of the relics, this did not affect the response of the people to the discovery of their saint. Miracles were reported, and while it is difficult to date some of them with precision, they all occurred in 1696 or perhaps 1697. The narratives include the same essential elements: first an illness and the failure of standard methods to cure the disease; then the command to seek the healing power of the water in the well of the crypt at San Pietro; then the cure. Colli, the Franciscan leading the investigation of the bones, recorded five accounts of miracles, though only four ended up in his final report. First there was the canon Carlo Emanuel Marcellino of San Nicolo della Moneta, who had been suffering from such violent headaches and dizziness for about three years that sometimes he would practically topple over while saying Mass; only by gripping the altar could he remain standing. His doctor thought he might have a stomach problem.[14] One day Carlo heard a voice speaking in Latin, which told him to go to where the body of St. Augustine had been found and to drink

13. Charles Taylor, *A true and perfect narrative of the strange and unexpected finding of the crucifix and gold-chain of the pious prince, St. Edward, the King and Confessor, which was found after 620 years' interment: and presented to His Most Sacred Majesty, King James the Second* (London, 1688). Even a fairly routine matter such as a reinterment of the illustrious dead could involve surprises. Dava Sobel has described the discoveries made at the 1737 reburial of Galileo in *Galileo's Daughter: A Historical Memoir of Science, Faith, and Love* (New York: Walker & Company, 1999), 366–68. In the early nineteenth century in the Pantheon in Paris, the remains of Rousseau and Voltaire, so it seems, were hidden for their own safekeeping and almost lost.

14. Bellelli, *Collectio actorum,* "Votum Josephus Caimottus" (1729), 2:87–88.

some of the water from the well behind the crypt altar. He did, and his headaches and dizziness disappeared. A more spectacular cure was that of another cleric, Francesco Bernardino Maio Solivetta, who on September 13, 1696, had been given up for dead by his doctor because of his high fever. In a sort of dream-delirium he heard St. Augustine speaking to him in Latin, telling him that if he were to drink from the water at the well next to where the saint's body had been found, he would be cured. He staggered to the well, drank the water, and his fever left him. The next day he sang the *Te Deum,* and by September 23 he had completely recovered.[15]

Another cure was performed on a sixteen-month-old boy named Giuseppe, the son of Anna Francesca Valle and Paolo Sala Pelizaro. The baby was sick with a fever, and his mouth had been infected with a foul-smelling ulcer for some three months. From birth he had had trouble attaching to his mother's breast; she had experienced a great deal of pain while nursing. When she heard that the saint's body had been found, she went to the crypt and prayed for six days straight. During the night of the sixth day, while she was sleeping and nursing her son, St. Augustine appeared to her in a vision. He was dressed as a bishop and looked exactly like his picture as it appeared at the entrance of the cathedral. Speaking to her in Italian, he told her to take her son the next day and cleanse his mouth with the water from the well located behind the crypt altar. On the following day it rained continuously and she decided to remain home. That night, with more than a note of impatience in his voice, the saint appeared again and told her, rain or no rain, to go to San Pietro the next day without fail to take advantage of the sacred water of the well. And go she did.[16] The next day, in the presence of the sacristan, she washed out her son's mouth and, for good measure, used the same water to cleanse her breasts. Her son's infection was promptly cured.

15. Water and wells were frequently associated with marvelous cures. Paola Vismara Chiappa, *Miracoli settecenteschi in Lombardia: tra istituzione ecclesiastica e religione popolare* (Milan: Istituto Propaganda Libraria, 1988), 47–61, describes near-contemporary claims of miraculous cures performed in Lombardy with water from a location near an object held to be sacred.

16. Saints in these kinds of stories were typically very insistent on their wishes' being carried out; patience was not expected from a saint who was anxious to bestow a blessing and perform a miracle. See Aron Gurevich, *Medieval Popular Culture: Problems of Belief and Perception,* trans. János M. Bak and Paul A. Hollingsworth (Cambridge: Cambridge University Press, 1988), 49–50. Later I will describe how, in a dream-vision, Augustine instructed Ferdinando Leva, a Canon Regular, to cease disputing the authenticity of the bones.

The fourth case was that of thirty-two-year-old Magdalena Massarola, who was married to Carlo Antonio Marconi. She had suffered from an extreme case of sciatica for seven months and had become so bent over that only with great difficulty could she ascend to the second floor of their house. Now she had become bedridden. When she heard of the discovery of the bones, she started praying every night to St. Augustine. One night the saint appeared to her and, speaking in Italian, told her to obtain some of the water from the well behind the altar where his relics had been found. Her husband, who was with her when the saint appeared to her, had seen nothing and laughed at her, saying she had lost her mind. Despite his ridicule—or perhaps this is a different version of the story—the very next day he carried her to the cathedral, bringing twenty soldi for a Mass, and went to the crypt. She applied some of the water to her back and said five Our Fathers and five Hail Marys; her back pain began to lessen. It is interesting to note that in most of the published versions the skepticism of the husband is not mentioned; it does not appear in the 1728 volumes summarizing the controversy or in the *Acta sanctorum* 1743 life of Augustine.[17]

Other miracles were related to Colli by the Contessa Gambarana, but he chose not to include her stories in his final accounts of verified miracles. Perhaps there were insufficient witnesses; more likely, the cures that she described were more difficult to distinguish from the normal operations of the human body recovering from illness, or simply from a patient's good fortune. He did, however, include her experiences in one of his manuscript accounts discussing the authenticity of the bones. We do not know if Colli wrote up her story for the sake of completeness or on the advice of others, or if he had momentarily decided to yield to the enthusiasms of an importunate, rich, and socially prominent patron. In any event, Colli's four cases have a nice parallelism: two males who are clergy, and two married women. None of them was involved with any significant aspect of public life. And, in contrast to contemporary eighteenth-century apparitions of the Virgin Mary, none of the females was unmarried or a child.[18]

17. Colli, *Responsio,* 91–94. *Acta sanctorum,* t. 6 Augusti (1858 ed.), 378. The cure of Suor Giovanna Margherita Campaniga in the mid-eighteenth century has interesting parallels with the examples in Pavia; see Chiappa, *Miracoli settecenteschi,* 147–58.

18. Chiappa, *Miracoli settecenteschi.* In many of the cases described by Chiappa, the miracles were seldom ratified by the clerical investigators. The Pavian case was unusual in that it had ecclesiastical support.

Colli properly documented his four miracles, and they have been accepted as authentic. These kinds of miracles were part of the social memory associated with the normal activities of a patron saint. The contessa is the only woman of the local nobility who participated in the investigation of the bones' identity. Her story and those of the other two women concern the home, family, and children, and thus follow the traditional patterns of such narratives.

Anna Francesca Valle, whose son was cured after a visit to the newly discovered relics in San Pietro, had seen St. Augustine in a dream-vision as a bishop who spoke Italian. Her image of Augustine was as a bishop, just as he was depicted in his image at the cathedral. One would be hard-pressed to find an artistic representation of Augustine made by a Renaissance or baroque artist that did not portray him as a bishop. Her description was not very different from that of Catholic religious scholars of this time whose impression of Augustine came from a knowledge of his books. For them too he was a bishop. The story of *The Confessions* told how Augustine had become a bishop. The most important reason to read his work was to learn how Augustine had become so. For these readers, Augustine had written the book to describe how his previous life experiences had prepared him to take on this traditional role in the administration of the Christian Church. Such a motive is scarcely intelligible to readers in our time, when few dream of a career path culminating in being appointed a bishop.

Ferdinando Leva and the other clerics who heard Augustine speak to them in Latin do not specify the visual cues, if any, that reassured them who their interlocutor was. Clothing was often a decisive element in similar accounts of visions. But for them, Augustine was not a generic bishop figure with a miter. Their Augustine had an identity as the prototype of their abbot; the members of the Canons Regular and the Augustinian Hermits shared this conception. Pavia's bishop, as they well knew, had his seat a ten minutes' walk away at the Duomo. Their Augustine was an abbot who, instead of a miter, wore the habit of their order. For these men, the text of Augustine that linked them to him was *The Rule*, and for most of these monks this was probably all the Augustine they ever read.[19]

19. There may have been some knowledge of Erasmus' claim that *The Rule* had originally been written by Augustine for a female monastery. Today this view has been substantially

For anyone living in Pavia, Augustine was a patron whose spiritual beneficence might be experienced by those who prayed to him. The workers who found Augustine's bones and saw the letters on the marble box had participated in this saint's sacred history, the mysterious eternity of myth. They had become part of Augustine's story. For them the acceptance of the bones as sacred appears to have been a straightforward matter. Augustine was their sacred protector, the patron of the people of Pavia, and a guarantor of the well-being of their city. It may be wondered whether the writings in the subsequent controversy affected the women and men who experienced the miracles, the workers who found the bones, or their friends in the Pavian community. Perhaps this transcendental experience was enriched by what was written about their saint's relics, and the presence of such writings may have enhanced or refined their perceptions and memory of the event. It is possible that reading or hearing of these events from printed texts supplemented the symbolic thinking involved in the workmen's recognition of themselves as taking part in their patron saint's life story. The exaltation that they probably experienced at the Invention would not be commemorated by the work of artists. What are recorded in Pavia are the contemporary arguments about the bones' authenticity and the testimony of witnesses. Other comparable examples make it tempting to assume that these Pavians experienced a communal wonder and amazement at the strange, awesome, sometimes playful powers manifested by a patron saint. In the medieval period such an event would typically result in displays of the energy and confidence felt by the local regime and its secular rulers as they humbled themselves before their patron saint. By making their prestige and authority subservient to their patron, they founded anew a political legitimacy based on the state's mastery of and reverence toward the relics of their patron. In Pavia we have the statements of the workmen and those who experienced miraculous cures; we can read the essays and polemics prepared by scholars and religious leaders. The only memorials of the event are the printed texts that celebrated it.

These Augustines are not our Augustine. These types or roles of bishop, abbot, and patron saint are alien to our experience. For us Augustine is an

---

refuted. See Adolar Zumkeller, *Augustine's Ideal of the Religious Life,* trans. Edmund Colledge (New York: Fordham University Press, 1986), 284–85, 297–98.

individual, and especially a writer of great books. He is a part of our intellectual tradition, required reading in some undergraduate curricula; he is an author whose works we might consult for spiritual illumination, consolation and guidance, and information about what it was like to live and learn in North Africa and Italy in late antiquity. A few Europeans of the late seventeenth century would have shared some of these attitudes, but for them Augustine's books and theological positions would have been more fundamental. Most who had an interest in his thought and writing associated his career and reputation with very different stories than the ones we have inherited. Augustine, especially for Catholics, was connected to dogma and to their experience of religious practice and the rituals of their church. His was a symbolic presence. For most Pavians he was also a real presence in their lives, but not because of anything he had said or written.

We do not know whether any of the laity in Pavia who followed the quarrel about Augustine's relics were prompted to learn more about the saint by reading his works. If such an interest existed, no publisher in Pavia saw a sufficient market to reprint any of them. This could mean that there was a sufficiency of his writings already available, not that there was any lack of interest. The only work of Augustine's printed in Pavia in the seventeenth and eighteenth centuries was the *Regula,* the Augustinian *Rule* for the monastic life. Nearby in Piedmont, in 1709, the Maurist edition of *De civitate dei* and the *Enarrationes in Psalmos* was printed in Vercelli, a city beyond Mortara on the road to Turin. Augustine's works certainly were available in Pavia. The library at San Pietro had been open to the public since the middle of the seventeenth century, but there is no evidence to indicate that it was a center of intellectual activity.[20] From a fifteenth-century book list we know that the Canons possessed seven manuscripts of Augustine's works, including a *Confessions* and a *City of God.*[21] People living in Pavia may nevertheless have found it difficult to buy the specific works of Augustine in Latin that they wanted.

The market for a printed book at this time was limited for the most part

20. Rodolfo Maiocchi and Nazerino Casacca, *Codex diplomaticus Ord. E.S. Augustini Papiae* (Pavia: C. Rossetti, 1905–15) 5:64–65. Among the library's rules was that anyone who stole a book was subject to excommunication.

21. Franco Borlandi, "Biblioteche pavesi del Quattrocento," *Bollettino della Società pavese di storia patria,* n.s. 1 (1946). Cipolla, *Literacy and Development in the West,* 108 (citing Quadri), reports that in the 1820s, the University Library in Pavia contained fifty thousand volumes.

to its local region; most printed material was not distributed abroad. Over time, however, certain editions and authors had a wide distribution. Evidence of this can be found in one of the most curious bibliographic ventures of the late seventeenth century, the *Biblioteca volante* (The flying library) of Giovanni Battista Cinelli. Cinelli traveled around to Italian cities, surveyed their libraries, and sought out the bibliographic rarities contained in them. He then published a book list of what he had found of interest in these libraries, frequently adding comments about the significance of specific editions. The lists were published in Italian book review journals of the late seventeenth and early eighteenth centuries. The reader of these book lists, some twenty of which were published, could construct Cinelli's vision of the ideal special collection. He usually included the place of publication, and this information alone makes clear that northern Europe's greatest publishing projects of the fifteenth and sixteenth centuries reached a wide area. Even obscure volumes traveled vast distances. Although there is anecdotal evidence, and we can make inferences from the book lists of private libraries about the used book trade, we have little definitive information about the presence of Augustine's works in the used book market in Pavia or Milan.[22]

For anyone who was interested and had the necessary cash, the 1690s was one of the most exciting decades in the printing history of Augustine's works. The Benedictines of the Congregation of St. Maur (they are often referred to as the Maurists or the Maurist Fathers) completed their great edition of his writings under the editorship of Jean Mabillon.[23] The first volume had been published in 1679, and the final volume appeared in 1700. The first ten volumes contained Augustine's writings; the eleventh consisted of his life as written up by Possidius soon after Augustine's death, and a Latin translation and revision of the biography composed in French

22. Biblioteca Nazionale di Pavia (hereafter BNPav), Mss. Ticinensis 33, "Catalogus librorum qui continenter in hac bibliotheca Santi Petri in Coelo aure Papiae 1750," lists only one Augustine title; there were six works of Aristotle, a Dante, the poetry of Bembo, a St. Theresa volume, and many works of theology. This list is of the printed books in the Hermits' library; it was the Canons' library that contained the Augustine manuscripts.

23. Michael M. Gorman, "The Maurists' Manuscripts of Four Major Works of Saint Augustine with Some Remarks on Their Editorial Techniques," *Revue bénédictine* 91 (1981), 238–79; A. M. P. Ingold, *Histoire de l'édition bénédictine de Saint Augustin avec le journal inédit de Dom Ruinart* (Paris: Augustin Marie Pierre, 1903). The Maurist editors were more interested in how textual variants might affect the interpretation of Augustine's thought than in the manuscript texts themselves.

by Tillemont for his own *Memoires pour servir à l'histoire ecclesiastique des six premiers siecles.*[24] Tillemont, who died in 1698, did not supervise the translation. Among the accomplishments of his biography was that it placed Augustine's writings in the context of his entire intellectual production: in his narrative Tillemont incorporated the sermons that Augustine delivered and the letters that he wrote, using them both to explain events in the saint's life and to provide a context for the books and other writings Augustine undertook. Tillemont studied the Maurists' edition and valued their dating of the letters and sermons; he used them to enrich his understanding of how Augustine's thought had developed and how he had presented his views to a variety of audiences.[25]

The Maurists' text of Augustine was the first major scholarly edition since the sixteenth-century edition prepared by the Catholic scholars of Louvain; that edition had been published by Plantin in Antwerp in 1577. Amerbach had printed the first complete edition of Augustine's works in Basel in 1506. Erasmus, in part to silence the complaints that he did not know his Augustine, edited the next one, Froben's 1526 Basel edition.[26] Editions of the complete works were published in Augsburg in 1537, in Paris in 1541, and Lyon in 1561.[27] The first complete works printed in Italy appeared in Venice in 1550 and 1558; the 1570 Venetian edition did not rely on Erasmus' text. The aim of its editors was to reassert that Augustine possessed pure Catholic credentials and had not slipped into heretical doctrine—an implicit criticism of Erasmus' edition, whose orthodoxy they apparently distrusted. Even after the appearance of the Louvain edition, the Venetians published their version once more. The 1577 Louvain edition became the major edition for the seventeenth century. It was reprinted in Geneva in 1596 and 1610, and it appeared in Cologne in 1616.

24. Goulven Madec, "Les 'Annales Augustiniennes' de Lenain de Tillemont et la 'Vita S. Augustini' des Mauristes," in *Troisième centenaire de l'édition Mauriste de Saint Augustin: communications présentées au colloque des 19 et 20 avril 1990* (Paris: Institut d'études Augustiniennes, 1990), 215–33, esp. 233.

25. On Tillemont, see two works by Bruno Neveu: *Un historien à l'école de Port-Royal: Sébastien Le Nain de Tillemont (1637–1698)* (The Hague: Martinus Nijhoff, 1966), and "Sébastien Le Nain de Tillemont (1637–1698) et l'érudition ecclésiastique de son temps," in *Érudition et religion aux XVIIe et XVIIIe siècles* (Paris: Albin Michel, 1994), 93–104.

26. Four more editions of his edition were published in Basel, the last in 1569.

27. In Paris there were also editions in 1555 and 1571, but Lyon came to dominate the French market with editions in 1565, 1570, 1580, and 1586.

The Louvain edition was printed in Paris in 1586, 1613, 1635, and 1651. An edition appeared in Lyon in 1664 and in 1693, while the Maurist edition was being completed. With a symbolism Augustine would have acknowledged and perhaps applauded, his works were frequently published in what was described as ten volumes, although the actual physical number of bound volumes in the set might be five, six, eight, fourteen, or seventeen.

The Paris firm of François Muguet printed the Maurist edition in eleven volumes from 1679 to 1700; a reprint was promptly made in Antwerp in 1700–1703. Another Parisian edition of the complete works was not to appear until 1835. The Venetians produced editions of the Maurist Augustine in 1729, 1756, and 1797 in nearby Bassano.[28] The text was printed in Naples in 1753. An edition appeared in Vienna in 1733.[29] Based on a rough estimate of the number of copies in each edition as less than a thousand, about 40,000 copies of the complete works of St. Augustine (some 250,000 volumes) would have appeared by the end of the eighteenth century. Basel dominated this production in the first part of the sixteenth century; Lyon printed the most editions until the end of the century. Paris dominated the seventeenth century, publishing both the Louvain and the Maurist editions. Editions of Augustine's complete works became the province of the Italians, especially Venetians, in the eighteenth century. This geographical distribution of editions is an indicator of interest in his thought, the presence of a readership with disposable income, and the saturation of markets. Apparently the Parisian market for Augustine's complete works disappeared as the Benedictines printed their volumes; the Louvain and St. Maur editions did not seem a good risk to French publishers of the eighteenth century. The survival rate of the Augustine volumes into the twentieth century is much higher than that of pamphlets and broadsides, which would have appeared in much greater numbers. This was not due solely to the intrinsic merit of the texts. The Augustine volumes were frequently folio volumes. Their size made them almost the equivalent of

28. The 1729–35 edition of Augustine was published by Giambattista Albrizzi; this publication was supported by four hundred subscribers. See *Novelle della repubblica delle lettere* (November 3, 1731), 351. On Albrizzi's work and his relationship with Muratori, see Mario Infelise, *L'editoria veneziana nel '700*, 2d. ed. (Milan: Tipomonza, 1991), 52–61.

29. This list of complete editions and the figures given later about *The City of God* and *The Confessions* does not claim to be complete. It is a compilation of holdings taken from published national library catalogues, a number of on-line catalogues, and book reviews in seventeenth- and eighteenth-century journals.

pieces of furniture, their expense ensured that the original owners preserved them with some care, and their bulk made disposal awkward. Multivolume sets, even in a smaller octavo format, had a higher survival rate than pamphlets, since such sets had more prestige and resale value. Augustine was collectable. Short, popular works had a much briefer shelf life and often could not expect to find any interest in the used book market. Pamphlets and small books could also serve as a ready supply of kindling, linings for bread and pastry pans, wrapping paper, and blotters and wipes of a more humble kind.

The earliest books published were not complete editions of an author's works but separate titles. The printer Aldo Manuzio (in Latin, Aldus Manutius), working in Venice in the 1490s until his death in 1515, probably did the most to establish the idea that a set of complete works signified the respect owed to a classic author. And Manuzio's book-buying public also accepted the notion that the mark of a discerning reader was ownership of an author's complete production in the original language. The impact of this marketing strategy gradually transformed the publication of the classics printed in Greek and Latin. In the early history of printing, most Greek and Latin texts were published as individual volumes. And while the overall number of editions in the original language of most classical authors declined as time went on, the proportion of editions of complete works to individual titles increased. In large measure, editions of complete works of classical authors in the original language displaced the publication of individual titles by the eighteenth century, except for standard texts of the university curriculum. This had the effect of making the purchase of the classics in their original language an expensive proposition for a general reader who had an interest in Greek or Latin books. New editions of individual works in the original language were not moneymakers for publishers.

Those with limited funds for books would find only multivolume sets for sale or translations of individual titles available in new editions; those interested in an original-language edition of a specific text would have to turn to the used book market. Vernacular translations of the Greek and Latin classics did not at first compete for market share with texts published in the original language, but by the mid-sixteenth century, translations had surpassed the number of editions of the original. The number of French and English translations generally increased from the seventeenth to the eighteenth centuries; translations into Italian reached a peak in the 1560s; no new translations of many classic authors appeared until the eighteenth century. French and Italian translations almost always were published before a version was printed in English.

Individual titles and collections of selected works by Augustine appeared decades before the first complete edition of 1506. One of the first printed works attributed to Augustine, the *Sermones ad fratres in eremo,* was in fact a forgery prepared by Augustinian Hermits or their sympathizers. The first printing of *De civitate dei* (The city of God) in 1467 was the work of the illustrious German printer Pannaertz, who had set up a shop in Subiaco outside Rome. In terms of the number of editions, this would be Augustine's most frequently printed work over the next two centuries. At least seventeen editions of it appeared in the fifteenth century; eight editions of the Latin appeared in the sixteenth century, five in the seventeenth (one edition in Hamburg), and four published in Italy and one in Ingolstadt were printed in the eighteenth century. An Italian translation appeared in 1480; the next Italian edition did not appear until 1743 in Rome. A verse translation of parts of Book 1 was printed in 1745. The first French translation was published in 1486; three editions were published in the sixteenth century, five in the seventeenth, and three in the first part of the eighteenth century. Two English editions appeared in the early seventeenth century, and a Spanish translation was published in 1676. The publishing history of *De civitate dei* follows the general pattern exemplified by most classical texts published from the beginnings of printing to the early nineteenth century. One significant difference was that *De civitate dei* was seldom published in Protestant printing centers. For them, Augustine was no longer a Latin classic but already a Catholic religious author.

The publishing history of the *Confessiones* (Confessions) followed a pattern of its own. It was first published in Strasbourg, perhaps in 1470, and then Milan in 1475; editions followed in 1482 and 1483, and there were two more Strasbourg editions in 1489 and 1491. No other separate edition appeared until 1531. Eleven editions appeared in the sixteenth century and twenty-seven in the seventeenth century: Elzevir published an edition in Leiden in 1675; eight editions were published in Cologne; four in Lyon, the last in 1691 by Anisson; and four were printed in Paris. Seventeen Latin editions appeared in the eighteenth century: nine appeared in Venice between 1691 and 1779; two were printed in Leipzig in the 1730s; and editions appeared in Augsburg in 1763, Paris in 1776, and Madrid in 1790. The first translation was into Spanish, published in 1554 in Salamanca. Selections were printed in Antwerp in 1555, and then the entire work in 1556, 1586, 1596, 1613, and 1674. Three editions appeared in the eighteenth century. An Italian translation was printed in 1564 and 1595; it was published again in 1620 in Milan; and four seventeenth-century editions appeared in Rome. A new translation appeared in Palestrina in 1723, and thirteen Italian translations appeared in the area of Venice between 1747 and 1777. The first French translation was in 1582; eighteen editions appeared in the seventeenth century, and twenty appeared between 1709 and 1763. French readers in the seventeenth century could choose between that published by the Jesuit René de Cerisiers (the first edition was dated 1662) and the Jansenist version of Arnauld d'Andilly (first published in 1656). A less partisan translation was prepared at the end of the century by Philippe Dubois Goibaud, a member of the Académie Française; it was first printed in 1687. Jacques Martin, a Benedictine of St. Maur, published another translation in 1743. The first English *Confessions* was published in 1620 in Paris by a Catholic; a Protestant edition correcting the papist version appeared in 1631; six editions appeared in the seventeenth century and four in the eighteenth. Four editions were printed in Ireland between 1770 and 1809. The first translation to appear in America was published in Baltimore in 1834. A Dutch translation was published in 1715, and German translations were printed in 1673, 1728, 1760, and 1798.

The *Confessions* received the greatest numbers of editions in the handpress period in France from the age of Louis XIV until the end of the Seven Years' War in 1763, and in Venice in the late eighteenth century when the republic was reevaluating its historical and political foundations. The development of these readerships for the *Confessions* in Paris and later in Venice can be connected to other patterns and intellectual trends. These readers appear to have had the traditional interest in its story of how this man, Augustine, became a bishop; to become a bishop was of course a religious act, and also required the individual to define himself in relation to his secular community. The change in readership indicates moments in which the *Confessions* began to develop a life of its own, to be read as a text independent of the rest of Augustine's works, and to attract readers who read nothing else of Augustine except the *Confessions.* It was only in 1645 that independent editions of the *Confessiones* surpassed the number of printings of *De civitate dei.* Just based on numbers of editions published in the sixteenth century, *De doctrina Christiana* might have been judged Augustine's second most important work, after *De civitate dei.*

Beginning with the mid-seventeenth century, readers and book buyers began to accept or make the judgment that the *Confessiones* was the quintessential Augustinian work. Except for some selections of *De civitate dei,* the rest of his corpus might be left for the specialist. Gibbon could baldly state, in 1789, that "my personal acquaintance with the Bishop of Hippo does not extend beyond 'The Confessions' and 'The City of God.'"[30] Such an admission would have discredited an individual as a serious scholar a century before. In the 1690s, no one thought it odd that Michelangelo Fardella, a Cartesian and promoter of the experimental method of Galileo, would publish an essay on Augustine's conception of the soul, *Animae humanae natura ab Augustino detecta* (The nature of the human soul as disclosed by Augustine).[31] Fardella's book was a commentary on Augustine's *De immortalitate animae* (Concerning the immortality of the soul), and on Book 10 of *De Trinitate* (Concerning the Trinity), *De quantitate animae* (Concerning the quantity of the soul). The editors of the Venetian book review journal *Minerva* believed this work to be of general interest and serialized it in their journal.

Other of Augustine's texts have interesting printing histories of their own. Several, like *De correptione et gratia,* are part of the controversy that developed around the issue of divine foreknowledge, divine grace, and free will. Erasmus and Luther engaged each other on the subject without much shared understanding or goodwill; Calvin was notorious for his clarity on the connection between God's will, His knowledge, and the free choice available to the individual human being. The Council of Trent, it was thought, had with some circumspection defined the differences of the Catholic position from that of its major Protestant rivals without rejecting, fa-

30. Edward Gibbon, *The History of the Decline and Fall of the Roman Empire,* ed. David Womersley (London: Penguin, 1994), 2:285 (chap. 33, n. 28). It should be pointed out that Gibbon's notes refer to other of Augustine's works; what he may mean is that these two were the only books he read through rather than simply using them as sources for specific bits of information. His other citations often derive from references made by other scholars.

31. Donatella Lauria, *Agostinismo e cartesianismo in Michelangel Fardella* (Catania: Giannotta, 1974).

voring, or adopting the vocabulary and terminology of the followers of either Augustine or Aquinas. The work that brought Augustine's view on this issue to center stage in seventeenth-century religious discourse was Cornelius Jansen's 1640 *Augustinus,* published two years after Jansen's death. This work was an explication of Augustine's thought on the issues of faith, works, grace, God's knowledge, and human freedom. Jansen, that is, his own printed statements, indicate that he believed his work was an honest interpretation of Augustine's meaning, which, as he saw it, was not in conflict with the statements made at Trent. Nevertheless, equally well-meaning Jesuits found, if not actual heretical statements, heretical intent in his text and concluded that the meaning of his teaching deserved condemnation. Most Jesuits, especially those doubting Jansen's candor, interpreted Jansen's thought (most had not read his book) as an attack on the ethical teachings and values promoted by the Jesuits in their books and in their school curricula. Jansen's dense and difficult work was notoriously little read, much talked about, and portrayed in the most extreme terms. The conflict between the Jesuits and the Jansenists is remarkable in the annals of the history of theological controversy; it made a significant contribution to the modern historical and literary imagination.[32]

The edition of Augustine on which Jansen had relied was that prepared by the scholars of Louvain. The theological discourse about Jansen's interpretation acquired a different standing when the French royal administration concluded that this controversy threatened to undermine the unity of their kingdom. Louis XIV's regime openly supported the contentions of the Jesuits and labored to destroy their rivals. When the Congregation of St. Maur announced its aim to prepare a new edition of St. Augustine, it was clear that this would place unusual pressure on the editors from the various factions within the Church and the French state. It was known that certain of Jansen's interpretations depended at times on specific textual readings or editorial interpretations made by the Louvain

32. See Leszek Kolawkowski, *Chrétiens sans église: la conscience religieuse et le lien confessionel au XVIIe siècle,* trans. Anna Posner (Paris: Gallimard, 1969), and *God Owes Us Nothing: A Brief Remark on Pascal's Religion and on the Spirit of Jansenism* (Chicago: University of Chicago Press, 1995). See also A. J. Abercrombie, *The Origins of Jansenism* (Oxford: Oxford University Press, 1939). Pascal's *Provincial Letters* taught theological irony to the eighteenth century, and its milieu promoted and perhaps inspired the remarkable passions and ambition imagined by Stendhal for his character Julian Sorel. Zbigniew Janokowski, *Cartesian Theodicy: Descartes' Quest for Certitude* (Dordrecht: Kluwer Academic Publishers, 2000), describes the relations between Descartes's metaphysical projects and Jansenism and Augustine.

editors. Would the Benedictines change these and thus favor the Jesuit interpretation? Or would they try to embarrass the Jesuits and humiliate Louis XIV? The Maurist edition earned a grudging respect from members of both sides in the controversy because of its resolute adherence to the principle of establishing what could be ascertained as fact, and to forgo or set aside personal opinion and belief.[33] Some of the editorial decisions favored the Jansenists, others supported the Jesuits. Moderation and restraint had a limited appeal in such a context; the controversy was so far advanced that evidence and goodwill counted for much less than a strongly held opinion. And, after all that energy had been invested, the core argument was scarcely capable of being resolved by the interpretation of a text.

The Benedictine edition proved not to be the common point from which both sides could reexamine their differences and begin a discussion aiming at reconciliation. The Maurist attempt to limit the debate to a discussion of the principles of textual interpretation had few charms and required a specialist's knowledge of the principles of palaeography and the historical world of late antiquity. The issues on which the Jesuits and Jansenists disagreed were fundamental; what the controversialists sought was simplification, not appreciations of complexities. Tillemont's biography was too long, too rich, and too moderate in its discussion of human free will and God's fiat. The continuing quarrel of the Jesuits with the Jansenists in the eighteenth century proved that the controversy could continue just as well without Augustine's text. And the political aspect of the controversy added immensely to its interest and bitterness.

How was an interested reader able to get a handle on the crucial issues? There was the serious doctrinal issue of grace and salvation that ought to be described, but for someone who hadn't grown up with the quarrel there was a need for a nuanced explanation of the convoluted legal and religious politics of the French monarchy and that of the papacy as well. Reading *The Confessions* or any of Augustine's works would scarcely serve as an introduction to these problems, and biographies of Augustine and shorter works in collections of saints' lives would not help either. Not many would want to read long Latin treatises explaining Jesuit theories of casuistry, and no thoughtful reader would imagine that Pascal's piquant *Provincial*

33. For a study of their editorial work, see Georges Folliet, "Les méthodes d'édition aux XVIe et XVIIe siècles à partir des éditions successives du 'De correptione et gratia,'" in *Troisième centenaire de l'édition Mauriste de Saint Augustin*, 71–102.

Letters offered anything like an impartial summary of the issues. At the end of the seventeenth century, a new scholarly resource appeared that served in some measure as the reference work for this controversy and Augustine's place in it. This work was Pierre Bayle's *Dictionnaire historique et critique,* which was first published in 1697; a second revised edition was printed in 1702. Editions followed Bayle's death: both a French edition and an English translation were published even in the early nineteenth century. The work was especially popular in northern Europe, but copies were readily available in Italy as well. Bayle did not originate the biographical dictionary, though he made it fun to read. His *Dictionnaire* rapidly acquired a reputation among freethinkers and those who enjoyed a good laugh at the foolishness to be found in humanities scholarship and biblical studies of the previous two centuries. The *Dictionnaire* contained the biographies of the great philosophers, religious figures, and the poets and writers of antiquity and of modern times. The articles were often funny and iconoclastic, and sometimes they scandalized readers with their relentless ridicule of unexamined premises. A few articles appalled and entertained with their scatological humor and pornographic descriptions. Some were short, not more than a couple of sentences; the article on Spinoza, however, was equal in length to a monograph. Three to seven folio pages were typical for an article. On many pages of the dictionary, at the top, the reader finds several lines from the article itself; beneath it, usually covering more than three quarters of the page, are the footnotes, printed in smaller type and set out in double columns. In the margins around both the text proper and the footnotes are further references in an even smaller typeface. Its appearance might suggest a parody of the erudite texts of the age, though I think Bayle valued without cynicism or skepticism the serious scholar's endeavor to find out the truth and the need to document sources properly. Among his aims was to chronicle the absurdities, pretensions, and limitations of the so-called wise as well as of the truly wise.

Bayle was a Protestant and a Calvinist of sorts and, like most intellectuals of his day, he was concerned with issues raised by the Jansenist-Jesuit debate. Many of the entries concerned the scholars and teachers involved in it.[34] It was no surprise that Bayle devoted an article to Augustine (the

34. Barbara Sher Tinsley, *Pierre Bayle's Reformation: Conscience and Criticism on the Eve of the Enlightenment* (Selinsgrove, Pa.: Susquehanna Press, 2001), relying on the *Dictionnaire,* describes Bayle's assessment of the major leaders of the Reformation.

vagaries of alphabetical order have it facing the end of the article on Averroës).[35] Bayle was amused by Augustine's unwholesome youth and sloppy education; he took some delight in pointing out Augustine's deficient knowledge of Greek. Bayle also noted that Averroës had no Greek and marveled at how well he had understood Aristotle without it. The article falling between those on Averroës and Augustine concerned Daniel d'Auge, who taught Greek in Paris in the second half of the sixteenth century. Greek in Bayle's view was not an ornament but an essential tool of the serious thinker. One of the few tenuous accomplishments of modern scholarship, he believed, had been the teaching and improved mastery of this ancient language.[36] The learned community of Europe, however, still had much basic work to accomplish; Bayle thought his ignorance of Arabic a failure in his own scholarly preparation. The absence of a scholarly edition of Averroës's great commentary on Aristotle was one example of how Europeans had failed in their duty to learning.

In his article on Augustine, Bayle made two major substantive points besides impugning Augustine's moral character. The more important was the argument that, despite his reputation as an orthodox religious thinker, Augustine had become an embarrassment to the Catholic Church. Taking a position that one may describe as more ingenious than true, he argued that St. Augustine's theology of free will and predetermination had, in fact and despite appearances, been rejected and declared heretical by the Council of Trent.[37] Jansen had, unfortunately perhaps, interpreted Augustine correctly. And the Jesuits were right about one thing: there was no difference between Jansen and Calvin on these issues. Bayle continued this observation, noting that St. Thomas Aquinas agreed with Augustine. The Council of Trent, he concluded had placed the Catholic Church in the position of either condemning a position no one held or declaring the teaching of Jansen, Calvin, Augustine, and the Thomists to be anathema. Such an interpretation was too delicious not to be savored; it had the right

35. Ruth E. Whelan, "The Wage of Sin is Orthodoxy: The 'Confessions' of Saint Augustine in Bayle's 'Dictionnaire,'" *Journal of the History of Philosophy* 26 (1988), 195–206; see also the comments in Tinsley, *Pierre Bayle's Reformation,* 209–18.

36. Pierre Bayle, *Dictionnaire historique et critique,* 3d ed., 4 vols. (Rotterdam: Michel Bohm, 1720), 1:389–94.

37. This argument has been revived for rather different purposes by Leszek Kolawkowski in *God Owes Us Nothing.*

kind of wit and raillery to deflect serious attempts at refutation. The influence of Bayle's clever twist shaped Gibbon's summary of Augustine's intellectual significance in *Decline and Fall of the Roman Empire.* As Gibbon phrases it, "The Church of Rome has canonized Augustine and reprobated Calvin. Yet, as the *real* difference between them is invisible even to a theological microscope, the Molinists [Jesuits] are oppressed by the authority of the saint, and the Jansenists are disgraced by their resemblance to the heretic."[38]

Bayle's other major observation concerned Augustine's use of allegory as an important way to interpret the meaning of Scripture. From other articles in the *Dictionnaire,* it was clear that this form of exegesis seemed unproductive to him. But instead of making the criticism himself, he quoted the French Catholic biblical critic Richard Simon, who also thought that allegory caused confusion for the interpreter and encouraged imprecise thinking. Simon believed that his interpretive approach, the use of a historical critical methodology, would enable one to read the original, literal sense of Scripture.[39] Bayle was interested enough in the difficulties this position caused Simon to return to the topic in his 1702 revision of the Augustine article. Bayle elaborated Simon's position and led from it into one of his favorite themes: that the proper way to show reverence to the great men of the past was not to repeat their views slavishly but to use human intelligence, the truth of Scripture, and reason to make judgments within the compass of our frail mental faculties.

The 1702 edition almost doubled the Augustine article in size. Besides continuing Bayle's observations on Simon, the other major additions to the article were comments on the new Maurist edition, the controversy it had created in Paris, and some observations on Jean LeClerc's attack on it in his 1702 *Appendix Augustiniana,* a supplement to the 1700 edition of Augustine published in Antwerp. LeClerc, a Protestant theologian and Arminian in his faith (a sect of Calvinism), adopted the pseudonym

38. Gibbon, *Decline and Fall of the Roman Empire,* 2:286 (chap. 33, n. 31).

39. Brevard S. Childs, "The Sensus Literalis of Scripture: An Ancient and Modern Problem," in *Beiträge zur Alttestamentlichen Theologie: Festschrift für Walther Zimmerli zum 70. Geburtstag,* ed. Herbert Doner, Robert Hanhart, and Rudolf Smend (Göttingen: Vandenhoeck & Ruprecht, 1977), 80–93. See also Hans Frei, *The Eclipse of Biblical Narrative: A Study in Eighteenth- and Nineteenth-Century Hermeneutics* (New Haven: Yale University Press, 1974).

Johannes Pheroponus in his attack on the Maurist text.[40] Bayle, with his eye for the incongruous, discussed one of LeClerc's queries as to whether into his old age Augustine had problems with hangovers caused by drinking too much wine (*Confessiones,* Book 10, chap. 31). The question concerned the distinction in meaning between *crapula* and *ebrietas,* or *crapule* and *ivresse.* LeClerc presented Augustine as a dissipated fellow. How was one to resolve such an issue? Bayle asked, and was St. Augustine really confessing to being a lush? His discussion reveals something of his method. Bayle observed that a resolution of sorts could be had by an appeal to the *Dictionnaire de la Académie Françoises,* but that would merely serve to confirm the definitions we already know. What was needed was to understand what these words meant at the time of St. Augustine. Furthermore, on making such an investigation, one must remember that poets and rhetoricians have a tendency to forget the thousand and one distinctions of meaning that the learned delight in teasing out of language. Bayle managed to put off making a final judgment but at the same time chided the Protestant scholar for overboldness and the Catholics for sidestepping a genuine issue.

It is worth commenting on one topic that Bayle chose not to discuss in detail in his essay on Augustine, though we know it was of great personal interest to him. In 1685, Louis XIV had publicly abolished the toleration that had been afforded to French Protestants since the 1598 Edict of Nantes had granted them protected status in France. Louis revoked the edict on the specious grounds that all Protestants had converted to Catholicism and hence it was no longer needed. Catholic theologians who aided Louis justified their vigorous methods by referring to the language used in the parable found in chapter 14 of the Gospel of Luke. A rich man, so the story went, planned a dinner party and invited his friends, but they all made excuses for not attending. Angered, he sent his servants to bring in the poor and travelers on the highway; referring to those strolling by in the street, the rich host instructed his household servants, "Compel them to come in"—"compelle intrare" in the Vulgate. Augustine had used this text when he justified his position to his parishioners that the Donatist heretics be readmitted and brought back into the Catholic Church. In 1686, Bayle had issued a pamphlet book on this topic, the *Commentaire philosophique*

40. LeClerc established his credentials as a textual critic in his *Ars critica,* which was published in Amsterdam in 1698.

sur ces paroles de Jésus-Christ: "Constrains-les d'entrer" où l'on prouve par plusieurs raisons démonstratives qu'il y a rien de plus abominable que de faire des conversions par la contrainte, et où l'on réfute tous les sophismes des convertisseurs à contrainte, et l'apologie que saint Augustin a faite des persécutions (A philosophic commentary on Jesus Christ's words "Compel them to come in," in which it is proved by many demonstrative reasons that there is nothing more hateful than to make conversions by force and which refutes the sophisms of those forcible converters, and the justification Augustine made for persecution). Even Christians cannot compel conscience, he argued.[41] Bayle made no direct mention of Augustine's interpretation of Luke in this article in the *Dictionnaire.* Instead, he followed the same indirect approach he had used with Simon and allegory. In footnote H, Bayle comments on the Protestant Jean Claude, who admired Augustine for everything except his willingness to use the penal laws of the state to enforce religious conformity. If he had lived a couple of years longer, Bayle noted, poor Claude himself might have come in for some rough treatment from his sovereign Louis XIV's zeal to compel his attendance. But even more scandalous, Bayle continued, were the radical Protestants, such as his former friend Pierre Jurieu, who had decided that state intervention was fine so long as it supported *their* interpretation and *their* conscience.

Bayle concludes the article by commenting on the new Amsterdam edition of Augustine's works. His source for this information was the *Nouvelles de la République des Lettres,* the book review journal that he had founded. The Amsterdam Augustine was a reprint of the Maurist edition, and it was to include, he noted, the interesting and excellent notes of Jean LeClerc. But at the last minute the decision was made to publish LeClerc's notes in a separate volume. The publishers feared that Catholics would avoid their edition if they had to buy the LeClerc notes as well. To maximize profits, and under the name of allowing readers a choice, the publishers issued the separate volume; now it was no longer an easy matter to juxtapose and compare the Catholic and Protestant commentary on Augustine's work. The requirements of the market were more important than the speculative advantages that might result from such scholarly exchange. Certainly Augustine's books had become a commodity. The book trade

41. J. C. Laursen, "Baylean Liberalism: Tolerance Requires Nontolerance," in *Beyond the Persecuting Society,* ed. J. C. Laursen and C. J. Nederman (Philadelphia: University of Pennsylvania Press, 1998), 197–215.

and the perception of what might sell may well explain why there was no modern edition of Averroës and no direct confrontation between Catholic and Protestant scholarship in the footnotes to Augustine's text. In Bayle's view, debates of this kind were one of the few places where knowledge could increase. Market forces, whatever else they were, Bayle noted in passing, were not supportive of the imaginative boldness and sympathy needed for scholarship to thrive.

TWO
The Problems with Augustine's Bones

As we have seen, the event of finding the remains of a holy person was part of a mythic narrative. Such discoveries were known as Invention, or *inventum*, the final piece of a narrative involving the posthumous careers of saints' bodies. The Invention was of particular importance in the spiritual life of Catholic Europe in the Middle Ages and in the early modern period. The first part of this narrative was called the Translation, the movement of the buried body or sacred object from one place to another. Such Translations were known in Hebrew, Greek, and Roman antiquity. The Translation of Joseph's mummified remains was one aspect of the Hebrew Exodus from Egypt. And there was the celebrated Translation of Cybele, Mater Deum Magna, the Great Mother, whose arrival at Ostia and journey to Rome was described in Book 4 of Ovid's *Fasti.* The act of Translation played an important role in medieval Christian Europe because many of the holy men and women, as well as sacred objects, had passed their lives or were buried in the eastern Mediterranean.[1] Fragments of the True Cross and bits of the nails used in the Crucifixion were once notoriously abundant in Europe; the Manger, supposedly translated from Bethlehem by the Virgin Mary to several Italian locations, was among the larger objects moved. The triumph of Islam in the seventh century, the growing interest in relics, the Crusades, and especially the sack of Constantinople in 1204 made it inevitable that these objects would travel to the West.

The posthumous career of St. Mark is an excellent example of the Translation and Invention narrative. Like much associated with Venice, it was stage-managed for maximum effect and social utility. The Venetian version of this story pattern illustrates a way to harmonize religion and

1. For an example of a Translation of relics to France a little after Augustine's transit, see, for example, Pierre Riché, "Translations de reliques à l'époque carolingienne: histoire des reliques de Saint Malo," in *Instruction et vie religeuse dans le Haut Moyen Age* (London: Variorum Reprints, 1981), 201–18.

secular authority without recourse to scriptural fundamentalism or the natural law tradition. The story was celebrated in a variety of mosaic styles decorating parts of St. Mark's Basilica in Venice, and in Tintoretto's cycle of four paintings commissioned originally for the Scuola Grande di San Marco. St. Mark had died a natural death, or was martyred (this was the Venetian preference), in Alexandria, Egypt, some time in the first century. It was believed in Venice that Mark had been introduced to his future home in the yet-to-be-built city of Venice by either a miraculous voyage or a vision. The tradition that St. Mark had founded churches in the nearby communities of Aquileia and Grado and had been their bishop prior to his mission to Alexandria was too convenient not to be incorporated into Venice's version of Mark's career (and as a justification for its imperial ambitions on the Adriatic coast). Venice needed to make the body and patrimony of St. Mark its own.

In 828 two Venetian merchants, Tribunus (or Buono di Malamocco) and Rusticus (Rustico da Torcello), doing business in Alexandria, managed to obtain Mark's body. They substituted the remains of St. Claudia for those of Mark and then sought to move his body from its tomb in great secrecy. A beautiful smell wafted over Alexandria upon the opening of his tomb. The Moslems had imposed an ordinance forbidding the export of relics; nevertheless, the wily Venetians tricked the Moslem customs inspectors by concealing the saint in a vat of pork. A depiction of this scene decorates the fifth doorway of St. Mark's west façade; a mosaic of the late seventeenth century, it shows the turbaned inspectors recoiling in horror before a basket containing the forbidden meat. Mark was thus translated across the Mediterranean, and four year's later the basilica was consecrated.[2] St. Mark's was built as the private chapel of the Doge, the ruler of Venice. This relationship of the saint, the basilica, and the Ducal Palace symbolized the remarkable cooperation between Venice's spiritual patron and its aristocratic leader.

But times change, and the outpouring of religious feeling that had greeted the arrival of Venice's patron saint gradually lessened. So the world goes: gradually the secular displaces the spiritual; the consequence is disorder. Sometime in the early tenth century, fearing that the political battles

2. There was no contemporary evidence to support this story. Tillemont, a Jansenist historian of the late seventeenth century, was the first to question the authenticity of Mark's relics.

taking place outside would spill into the cathedral, members of the clergy hid the relic for safekeeping. And, as in daily life, when one puts something away, the storage place can be forgotten. Knowledge of the whereabouts of St. Mark's relics was lost, and by the eleventh century they could not be located in the church. But a just proportion and true sense of spiritual values returned to the Venetians, and at the end of the eleventh century they rebuilt St. Mark's Cathedral. In 1094 they were ready to consecrate this, the third St. Mark's, the one we know today. But where was their patron saint? The city turned out to pray and fast, and after three days, the saint appeared in a dream and revealed that his body was in a sarcophagus that was standing upright in a column. The column miraculously opened, revealing the saint inside. St. Mark's body was found; the inventum had occurred. But this was no simple Invention; the Saint had actually intervened as if to make perfectly clear that there was a bond between himself, Venice, and its secular regime.

This harmony is the unambiguous message of the thirteenth-century mosaics of the south transept, which depict this scene. The artist emphasized the continuing validity of this message by representing contemporary political leaders in the place of the historical personages of the late eleventh century.[3] The image shows the Doge and the Venetian aristocracy leading the general rejoicing. True religious feeling had returned to the community. It would be naïve to assert that the mosaic portrays what any individual historical actor actually thought; the image presents a society that has forgotten political faction and class antagonisms. We see a community that has embraced the mythic memory of a unified city spontaneously rediscovering and embracing its patron saint. The aristocratic rulers of the city exhibit a proper humility before the city's patron-protector and a respect for the uncanny powers associated with him. St. Mark, the figure in the mosaic, implicitly confirms the recognition that their adoration of him is an expression of both individual inner piety and the cultural and

3. Otto Demus, *The Mosaics of San Marco in Venice,* vol. 1, *The Eleventh and Twelfth Centuries,* and vol. 2, *The Thirteenth Century* (Chicago: University of Chicago Press, 1984) 1:57–72, 2:27–44. See also Otto Demus, *The Mosaic Decoration of San Marco, Venice* (Chicago: University of Chicago Press, 1988), 193–204. Agnellus da Ravenna's ninth-century history *Liber pontificalis sive vitae pontificum Ravennatum* offered a methodology of historical reconstruction that could justify the belief that authentic reconstructions of the past can be accomplished using ideal types. See Thomas J. Heffernan, *Sacred Biography: Saints and Their Biographies in the Middle Ages* (New York: Oxford University Press, 1988), 142–68.

political ideals of the Venetian republic. The thirteenth-century mosaic of the Invention responds to the conception of the state-church relationship of its own day irrespective of what happened in 1094. The lack of evidence makes it difficult to determine what if anything happened involving St. Mark's relics in 1094, when the cathedral was reconsecrated. This artistic representation may well be a creative remaking of the historical past. But such is the power of images, symbols, ritual, and the patterns of stories that St. Mark's body was never lost again and has remained the most venerated relic in the city.

St. Augustine's posthumous career was more complicated than that of St. Mark and lacked the civic aspect so fully developed for the apostle's role in Venice. It was well known that Augustine had passed the last forty years of his life in North Africa; he died on August 28, 430, in Hippo, where he was bishop. Possidius, his biographer and friend, describes his last days in detail. At some subsequent date, but before the early eighth century, Augustine was translated from North Africa to Sardinia because of threats of violence and fear of destruction to his remains. This is as precise as modern scholars are willing to get in determining the date of his first Translation.[4] One account tells us that on October 11 (others say that October 11 was when Augustine was buried in Pavia), in some year of the late fifth or early sixth century (508 has some support), St. Fulgentius, bishop of Ruspe, reached Sardinia with St. Augustine's body.[5] Fulgentius had run into trouble with North Africa's Vandal rulers because of his too forthright defense of orthodox Christianity against their Arian heresy. The tradition tells us, and there seems no reason to doubt this (though there is no positive evi-

4. Jan T. Hallenbeck, *The Transferal of the Relics of St. Augustine of Hippo from Sardinia to Pavia in the Early Middle Ages* (Lewiston, N.Y.: Edwin Mellen Press, 2000), 156–81.

5. Our primary source of information about Fulgentius comes from a *Vita* written by a monk associated with him and the monastery Fulgentius founded at Cagliari in Sardinia. In the seventeenth century, the Jesuit Pierre-François Chifflet argued that the author was Ferrandus, a deacon of Carthage. This was accepted by Lapeyre in his 1929 edition of the text. Antonio Isola has contested this attribution in his 1987 Italian translation, *Pseudo Ferrando di Cartagine: Vita di San Fulgenzio* (Rome: Città Nuova, 1987), 5–8. The *Vita* makes no mention of Augustine's remains, nor does it affirm that Fulgentius had access to Augustine's library or that he took it with him to Sardinia. It is clear from his extant works that Fulgentius had access to a number of Augustine's writings. On Fulgentius' relation to Augustine's thought, see Bashuth Mapwar, *La polemique anti-arienne de St. Fulgence de Ruspe en Afrique du Nord (Ve–VIe siècles)* (Rome: N. Dominici-Pécheux, 1988).

dence to support it), that Augustine's body was kept in or adjacent to the Church of San Saturnius in Cagliari when it arrived in Sardinia. Fulgentius, according to one tradition, built his Sardinian church with a remnant of a piece of wood that Augustine himself had used, so the story went, to magically lengthen the main beam for one of his new African churches when the original beam proved to be too short.[6] There is some reason to believe that Fulgentius may have brought St. Augustine's library with him when he traveled to Sardinia. We know from the biography of Fulgentius prepared by his associate Ferrandus that he was recalled from exile, returned to North Africa, and then later returned to Sardinia; no explicit mention is made of transporting St. Augustine's body or his library on any of these trips.

In the early eighth century, Augustine's relics in Sardinia were endangered again, this time by pirates and Arab conquerors from North Africa. Sometime between 710 and 730, Augustine's body was translated from Sardinia to Pavia under the auspices of Liutprand, king of the Lombards. February 28 was the traditional date of this second Translation; the burial date of St. Augustine in San Pietro was October 11. We are told that Liutprand paid a huge sum for the body—some said sixty thousand gold pieces—but it is not certain to whom the money was given.[7] Some speculate it was a ransom paid to Moslems who had captured the relics, others presume it was a deal worked out with local Sardinians, and a third possibility is that members of the North African (that is, Byzantine) clergy living in Sardinia received the payment. Some denied that there was a payment and regarded the Translation as a spontaneous gift. Most of the accounts favor the view that the exchange was a transaction between Christians. In Sardinia there was a story, subsequently discredited, that the body had been sold, but that Sardinia had kept the saint's garments. Another version asserted that Augustine's relics spent a substantial time in Genoa before the body's final removal to Pavia; but no contemporary

6. This kind of power was attributed to numerous saints. See Aron Gurevich, *Medieval Popular Culture: Problems of Belief and Perception,* trans. János M. Bak and Paul A. Hollingsworth (Cambridge: Cambridge University Press, 1988), 45; his specific example is St. Lawrence.

7. On the issue of the commerce in relics, see two works by Patrick Geary: "Sacred Commodities: The Circulation of Medieval Relics," in *The Social Life of Things: Commodities in Cultural Perspective* (Cambridge: Cambridge University Press, 1986), 169–91, and *Furta sacra: Thefts of Relics in the Central Middle Ages* (Princeton: Princeton University Press, 1978).

evidence supports such a claim either. Genoa, though, was the probable port used to receive Augustine's relics when they were transported from Sardinia.[8] The documents describing the Translation do not make it clear why Liutprand selected Pavia to be Augustine's home. Pavia was the capital of the Lombard kingdom, but Augustine had no known connection with Pavia. In nearby Milan were the relics of his teacher Ambrose; he had received baptism in Milan, had lived in Rome, and his mother had died in Ostia. Perhaps Liutprand sought to discipline or even to humble the Milanese, as has been suggested by Jan Hallenbeck.[9] The Translation derived from Liutprand's piety; once done, it may have figured nicely in the complex mix of diplomacy and warfare that Liutprand used to expand his kingdom in his dealings with the dukes of Spoleto and Benevento, the pope in Rome, and the Byzantine emperor's representative in Ravenna.[10]

Liutprand must have had some plan for housing such a significant relic. He had a special devotion to St. Peter. But we do not know whether he built San Pietro, remodeled an older church, or adapted some other preexisting structure.[11] The tradition elides these difficulties. The presence of Boethius' tomb in San Pietro has suggested that a chapel of some sort already existed; this would have been outside Pavia's walls. (Boethius had been executed in the early sixth century). We also do not know to which religious order Liutprand entrusted the relics or who was responsible for this new or remodeled church.[12] What is clear is that Liutprand was quite committed to this new dwelling for Augustine. Liutprand himself chose to be buried in the church: In the early twelfth century, during a period of

8. Robert J. Rowland, Jr., "The Sojourn of the Body of St. Augustine in Sardenia," in *Augustine in Iconography: History and Legend,* ed. Joseph C. Schnaubelt and Frederick Van Fleteren (New York: Peter Lang, 1999), 189–98. On Sardinia in general, see Robert J. Rowland, Jr., *The Periphery in the Center: Sardinia in the Ancient and Medieval Worlds* (Oxford: Archeopress, 2001).

9. Jan T. Hallenbeck, *Pavia and Rome: The Lombard Monarchy and the Papacy in the Eighth Century* (Philadelphia: American Philosophical Society, 1982).

10. Hallenbeck, *Transferal of the Relics of St. Augustine,* 183–200.

11. Ibid., 145–49, 100–107.

12. Liutprand built a number of religious and secular structures, especially in Pavia, which he envisaged as a New Jerusalem. See Stefano Gaspari, "Kingship Rituals and Ideology in Lombard Italy," in *Rituals of Power: From Late Antiquity to the Early Middle Ages,* ed. Frans Theuws and Janet Nelson (Leiden: Brill, 2000), 95–114, esp. 109–10 and 99.

rebuilding, Liutprand's remains were moved to their current location in the basilica near the entrance to the crypt.[13]

The relics of such an illustrious saint attracted a good deal of attention from prestigious visitors, including popes, emperors, and kings. A visit to Pavia and Augustine was a usual stop for medieval pilgrims in northern Italy.[14] His august presence, however, seems not to have greatly altered patterns of religious devotion in Pavia, nor did Augustine's renown transform local loyalties. Pavia already had a patron saint, St. Siro, who was the city's first bishop and a disciple of the apostle Peter; in fact, Siro had been the boy who helped the apostles with the distribution of the loaves and fishes and the subsequent gathering up of the fragments.[15] Siro's relics were in the Duomo, the cathedral of Pavia's bishops. Many believed that Siro had built a church dedicated to Peter, naming it San Pietro after his teacher. Even if this were true, it would not help much, since there were at least two churches and perhaps as many as four named for Saint Peter, built prior to Liutprand's arrival. Siro had another useful function: he allowed the Pavians to claim that their first bishop and first church antedated those of Milan. This was a factor in Pavia's long-standing desire for political independence from, and cultural preeminence over, its powerful neighbor. St. Siro remained the most important local religious figure in Pavia. Augustine's international reputation did not damage Siro's local primacy—certainly not in the long run.[16] Liutprand may have intended to connect Augustine with the Lombard kingdom, but Charlemagne defeated its empire at the end of eighth century. None of Pavia's subsequent rulers sought to connect their political authority to that of Augustine.

13. Benedikt Hackett, "San Pietro in Ciel d'oro, Pavia," in Schnaubelt and Van Fleteren, *Augustine in Iconography,* 199–222. See also Ezio Barbieri, "L'archivio antico del monastero di S. Pietro in Ciel d'oro di Pavia (Secoli viii–xii), *Bolletino della Società Pavese di Storia Patria,* n.s. 29–29 (1976–77), 37–74.

14. Giacomo C. Bascapè, "Le vie dei pellegrinaggi medievali attraverso le Alpi centrali e la pianura lombarda," *Archivio storico per la Svizzera italiana* 10 (1936), 5–45.

15. Cesare Prelini, *San Siro, primo vescovo e patrono della città e diocesi di Pavia,* 2 vols. (Pavia: Fusi, 1880–90).

16. Interesting examples of new saints introduced into medieval Italian cities in northern Italy from a later period can be found in André Vauchez, "Patronage of Saints and Civic Religion in the Italy of the Communes," in *The Laity in the Middle Ages: Religious Beliefs and Devotional Practices,* ed. Daniel E. Bornstein, trans. Margery J. Schneider (Notre Dame, Ind.: University of Notre Dame Press, 1993), 153–68; one example concerns the Augustinian Hermits in the town of Amendola, a small city in the Marches.

As with Mark, Augustine's relics were held in high regard for many years; but as with all things human, there was a decline of respect and reverence. Although it is extremely difficult to say when, knowledge of the precise location of his relics was forgotten. Some dated this as occurring as early as the ninth century. A few claimed that the location was never lost, but the traditional view accepted the disappearance. Positive knowledge of their location had ceased by the fifteenth century, though no occasion made the ignorance of the exact location of the relics a matter of embarrassment. In 1503, St. Augustine intervened on behalf of Pavia and freed it from a deadly plague; for this he was proclaimed one of the city's protectors. His continued presence was indicated by reports of periodic cures and expulsions of demons.[17] It seems fair to say, then, that if there was no precise knowledge of the location of his body, all concerned "knew" where it was until someone might chance to ask to be shown it. A variety of oral traditions about Augustine's Pavian history were in circulation prior to the Invention of 1695. The subsequent controversy over the bones' authenticity clarified some of these issues but also made it difficult to trace versions that differed from the official account, which was certified in 1728.

Despite the miracles and the publicity about the finding of the bones, there was no official celebration in Pavia because no agreement as to the identity of the bones was reached. Why not? Well, in an official sense the reason can be simply stated: the appropriate authorities were not persuaded that the evidence was sufficient to warrant such identification. The Hermits were enthusiastic about the discovery, and Michele Colli very quickly became an advocate of the relics' authenticity. The real reasons for the delay were what might be called political reasons rather than ones bearing on the substance of the case. The primary factor was the peculiar constitution of San Pietro in Ciel d'Oro. Two Augustinian religious orders, the Canons Regular and the Augustinian Hermits, were in the unusual situation of sharing the same church. Prior to the discovery of the relics, the relationship between the brotherhoods might best be described as an armed truce. When the bones were found in the course of a building project sponsored primarily by the Augustinian Hermits,

17. Augustine, in 1559, performed a miracle in Lima, Peru. *Acta sanctorum,* t. 6 Augusti (1858 ed.), 377–78, 384–85.

the Canons Regular could be expected to dispute their claim: and so it happened.

These religious orders shared San Pietro, they both followed the Rule of St. Augustine, and both considered him the founder and patron of their order. Their quarrel can be described as a quarrel of brothers, each claiming to be their father's favorite son. But this description would overly simplify the differences that separated these brotherhoods. The Catholic religious world was one of great diversity, and this was reflected in its monastic and other sacred foundations. By the seventeenth century, there were all sorts of religious associations. Some were centered on local parish churches or grand cathedrals; others were associated with a monastery. Most urban parishes sponsored lay religious societies called confraternities, and some monastic orders had created affiliate organizations of the laity known as "Tertiaries." Civic governmental bodies and craft guilds included a religious component as part of their principles of organization and purpose. They were linked to specific patron saints and also special religious devotions. This quarrel in Pavia concerned the two religious orders; confraternities were not a factor.

Religious orders had their own traditions. Each order had a uniform or habit and sometimes a distinctive hairstyle that made the members readily identifiable. Certain orders limited membership to those whose birth entitled them to a special social status. The Theatines, for example, accepted only nobles, though a dispensation of this requirement was possible. Many families had a tradition of enrolling some of their members in a specific order, and their place in the religious community would often mirror their family's status in the secular community. Authoritarian administration by an abbot was the norm, but the governance of some depended to a great extent on consensus. Certain orders, like the Alexian Brothers, had a mission with the urban poor, and were closely connected to their local secular community. Many engaged in some form of teaching; the Jesuits were particularly industrious at producing textbooks for all the subjects taught at a university. Some orders, such as the Dominicans and the Franciscans, specialized in preaching and hearing confessions. Some were isolated or independent entities; others were noted for their adherence to papal interests. Some earned their money by begging and tried to avoid any involvement with financial matters. Others supported their religious communities with an investment portfolio based on rents on farms, the sale of agricultural products, and other business transactions. A few had managed to be entrusted by the state with monopoly control over the import or export of certain commodities. Almost all eventually possessed substantial real estate holdings and lavish edifices decorated with artworks and other precious furnishings. At times a religious order might be identified with a particular theological position, a specific religious devotion, or some secular political concern. The French Oratorians, some thought, inclined toward Jansenism, though it would be more exact to describe them as fellow opponents of the teachings of the Jesuits.

The origin of an order was often connected with the spiritual leadership of an especially venerated individual—Benedict, Francis, Clare, Dominic, or Ignatius Loyola, for example. Sometimes these religious institutions seemed to appear spontaneously, in various locations, and without any charismatic founder. Such principles of origin, which the nineteenth century might call an organic growth, seemed incomplete and lacking in dignity to early modern sensibilities. A distinguished beginning point—an illustrious patron—was needed to found a proper institution. For example, the Carmelite order first appeared in the 1100s, perhaps in Syria; its members claimed that their monastic order was, however, of great antiquity and was originally created by the prophet Ezekiel. Papal approval of the Carmelite Rule in 1226 was viewed as an affirmation of venerable practice rather than an inauguration. San Pietro's Augustinian orders were of this kind, but that did not prevent both from tracing their order to St. Augustine.

The two orders that shared San Pietro held centrist positions on many issues. Neither had extreme views on poverty and the amount of fasting and physical discipline appropriate to the religious life. The Canons Regular regarded themselves as having the more aristocratic membership and as being more highbrow than the Augustinian Hermits. Both were governed by an abbot or prior. Modern historians date the origins of the Canons Regular to the late eleventh century, when a number of monasteries living under the Rule of St. Augustine were united under a more centralized administrative structure. The Third Lateran Council of 1179 made Augustine's Rule binding on the Canons Regular; the first documented connection between the Canons and the Rule has been traced to Rheims in 1067.[18] The Augustinian Hermits were given their name (Ordo

18. Adolar Zumkeller, *Augustine's Ideal of the Religious Life*, trans. Edmund Colledge (New York: Fordham University Press, 1986), 90–94.

Eremitarum sancti Augustini) and principles of organization in 1256 by Pope Alexander IV.[19] This bull brought together into one order some 180 religious houses.

Knowledge of this historical origin was not forgotten in the seventeenth century, but its significance was interpreted in ways that we might regard as tendentious. Both orders believed that they had been founded under the inspiration of St. Augustine and, furthermore, that Augustine not only was their spiritual founder but also had directly created their order himself. One of the orders had to have been founded first, and, depending on whether you favored the Canons or the Hermits, the first was the one most loved by Augustine. Augustine did establish a number of religious communities, and his writings indicate that he had reflected profoundly on the purpose of the religious life. Augustine made no mention of either the Canons or Augustinian Hermits, but this absence of evidence made its meaning clear according to the bias of the interpreter.

The great seventeenth-century historians of both orders presented their positions: Gabriel Pennotto published in folio his one-volume history of the Canons Regular in Rome in 1624; he was answered by Luigi Torelli's nine-volume history of the Augustinian Hermits.[20] Pennotto asserted that Augustine was the founder of the Canons Regular, though the actual origin of the Canons derived from the apostles themselves: Augustine modified the orders they had established and gave them a new Rule. The Canons dated their order to 391, when Valerius, the bishop of Hippo, approved Augustine's plan to join the duties of a priest with the routines of a monastic life and permitted Augustine to build a monastery around the garden adjacent to Valerius' church. This, according to Pennotto, was the first religious order Augustine founded, the Canons Regular. The hermit's life, or the life of a Hermit, he declared, would have been repugnant to him. Pennotto felt that he had to address the criticism of the order's rivals,

19. See, for example, Rafael Kuiters, "Licet ecclesiae catholicae," in *Augustiniana septimo exacto saeculo a magno unione MCCLVI–MCMLVI,* ed. Franciscus Roth and Norbertus Teeuwen (New York: Augustinian Historical Institute, 1956), 9–36.

20. Gabriel Pennotto. *Generalis totius sacri ordinis clericorum canonicorum Historia tripartita cuius in prima parte de clericali sanctissimi P. Augustini instituto, & habitu in seconda de origine, procursuque totius ordinis canonicorum regularium. in tertia de congr. canonic. salvatoris lateransi locupletissime disseritur* (Rome: Camera Apostolica, 1624). Luigi Torelli, *Secoli Agostiniani ovvero historia generale del sacro ordine Eremitano del Gran Dottore di Santo Chiesa S. Aurelio Agostino vescovo d'Hippona divisa in tredici secoli,* 9 vols. (Bologna: Gio Battista Vaglierni, 1659–86).

who claimed that the Canons led a luxurious lifestyle. Pennotto needed to be careful, however; it was important to stress the seriousness of the order's mission, but at the same time he did not want to discourage vocations. Yes, he conceded, some claim that no Canon could withstand the Hermits' rigorous life and destitution; but the Augustinian monastic life required that all property be communal, not that all wealth be given away. The Hermits, he noted, could not date from Augustine's times; the saint was never a hermit. The Hermits were a recent foundation. The twelfth-century prophet Joachim of Fiore, in fact, included the Hermits with the Franciscans as one of those new religious orders that marked the new age of the spirit. Torelli and the tradition of the Hermits preempted the Canons with a founding date of 387. Shortly after Augustine's conversion in that year, Alypius and Evodius, two of Augustine's African followers, joined him in an arcadian retreat to study the liberal arts at Cassiciacum, a country estate near Milan. They were the first Hermits. It was at this time that Augustine began wearing the distinctive and well-known black habit of the Hermits.

It should be noted that neither position was supported by positive evidence. To be sure, Augustine studied and contemplated at Cassiciacum, but there is no evidence that he created a community; a monastery was created in Valerius' garden, but there is no evidence to connect it with the Canons. The lack of proof connecting Augustine to these orders invited the forging of the appropriate documents. It is ironic but telling that among the first printed works of Augustine was a 1477 edition of a collection of letters which he was supposed to have written to some Augustinian Hermits; these forgeries probably dated from fourteenth-century Flanders. In 1484, Pope Sixtus IV, after listening to the arguments of the Canons and the Hermits, commanded that both sides keep silent on this issue. The rivalry between these orders nevertheless continued into the twentieth century.

In Pavia, as one might imagine, each order had its own version of the history of Augustine's body. It is difficult to reconstruct with certainty the fine points of their traditions concerning the history of Augustine's bones in Pavia prior to 1695. Some believed that an Augustinian order had taken care of Augustine's body since its departure from Africa; others thought that this stewardship began with the Translation to Pavia. But, this presumption was clearly in error, and corrected versions erased soon after the Invention. The conventions of historical narratives about religious houses required that there be no chronological gaps and that nothing be left unexplained from their beginning to the present. There must be no gaps in lists of abbots so that the apostolic succession may be continuous. It was, one might say, culturally unacceptable to leave any blanks in the story; the model was that of a genealogy in which there is continuity between generations, no ambiguity about paternity, and no unsavory ancestors. Another presupposition of this mode of thinking was that the founding moment was illustrious and complete; a fall was always possible, but the perfection of the beginning could not be surpassed. As for Liutprand's removal of Augustine to Pavia, everything had to have been done in accordance with traditional expectations of the seventeenth century. It would have been indecent for a king to bestow such a bequest in a casual manner, and since Liutprand was not a vapid man, his establishment of the cult of St. Augustine in Pavia must therefore have been carried out with attention to all the proprieties. Hence, given the unwillingness to admit that the evidence did not make clear who had cared for the relics, it was asserted that the Benedictines had held this trust from the first. This was inferred from the certain knowledge that Benedictines subsequently had this responsibility. The role of the Benedictines, however, while an essential piece of the story, had no part in the local oral tradition about the Translation.

It was known that the Emperor Otto I mentioned the Benedictines of Pavia in a letter in 947. We know, too, that San Pietro was included in the Cluniac reform at the end of the tenth century.[21] San Pietro itself was rebuilt to its present form in the early twelfth century; at the beginning of the thirteenth century, the church became enclosed within a new city wall.[22] But in the early thirteenth century things were not well with San Pietro's Benedictines, and it was at this time that Augustine's relics were handed over to the Canons. The reason for the change of caretakers was a scandal: the Benedictine monks had murdered Aldo, their abbot, sometime around 1220. The reasons given for the murder were Aldo's commitment to reform and his discipline of the monks under his charge. Pope Honorius III, himself a Canon, appointed Canons Regular from the nearby Congregation of Mortara to replace the Benedictines and to take

21. Giuseppe Casati, "La regola Benedettina e i monasteri benedettini di Pavia," *Bollettino della Società pavese di storia patria* 81 (1981), 96–116.

22. Bianca Dragoni, "Il comune di Pavia fra il mille e il milleduecento," *Bollettino della Società pavese di storia patria* 30 (1930), 1–113.

charge of the relics.[23] Their solitary possession of the church was to continue for about a century.

In the middle of the thirteenth century an order of Augustinian Hermits was established in Pavia at the church of Santa Mostiola; later it became a female monastery, and in the eighteenth century it was secularized and made into a school building. The Augustinians replaced a Dominican order that had been housed there; the Dominicans were explicitly forbidden to enter the Augustinian establishment.[24] The Canons Regular at San Pietro and the Augustinian Hermits at Santa Mostiola seem to have gotten on very well. The presence of another Augustinian order in town did not create a rivalry. The quarrels in Italian cities between the Guelph and the Ghibelline factions, the conflict between the papacy and the empire, and the transfer of the papacy to Avignon, the "Babylonian Captivity," vastly complicated the relationship of religious orders among themselves and with their secular communities.

In early 1327, during the pontificate of John XXII, these disputes became embedded in the spiritual life of San Pietro in Ciel d'Oro. John had received signal aid from Guglielmo da Villana (known in English as William of Cremona), the prior general (the title of the chief executive officer) of the Augustinian Hermits. He had vigorously supported the pope against Emperor Louis the Bavarian. Guglielmo had forcefully challenged the arguments of Marsiglio of Padova, the political theorist for the independence of imperial and other forms of secular power from the papacy. Guglielmo thought that the Hermits deserved a significant reward for such service and requested that his order have a role in the care of St. Augustine's relics. John seemed willing to grant the request but recognized that there were serious difficulties, given that the Canons Regular were already established at San Pietro. It is indicative of Pope John's rich and peculiar spirituality that he was willing to countenance the presence of two rival hegemonic entities sharing one ecclesiastical building complex.[25] The traditions of each order represented different approaches to the spiritual and religious life, and both had received official sanction. The enforced juxta-

23. Ludovico Muratori, *Annali d'Italia,* 3 vols. (Milan: Fratelli Ubicini, 1838), 3:335.

24. Rodolfo Maiocchi and Nazereno Casacca, *Codex diplomaticus Ord. E.S. Augustini Papiae* (Pavia: C. Rossetti, 1905–15), 1:1–2.

25. Ibid., 1:13–19 (January 20, 1327).

position of these rival approaches would occasion at the very least some kind of debate. As the pope seemed to recognize, even the most vigorous intellectual or clerical argument was not the same thing as social change or political revolution. While John might agree that the Church represented a unity, a specific church might be divided, each part being an individuality, autonomous and not reducible to the other. It would seem that a church divided could have the same moral authority and spiritual force as one that housed a single religious order. The bull dealing with this decision is a remarkable document prepared by one of the most subtle bureaucracies ever to have administered the affairs of state. It dealt with the probably unprecedented situation of compelling two different religious orders to share the same church by ignoring any of the potential difficulties. Proceeding as if there were no foreseeable problems in ordering the Canons Regular to hand over half of their church to the Hermits, the document continued, with the insouciance of the hardened bureaucrat, to explain that both orders were expected to share and cooperate on many matters, and at the same time each was to remain autonomous and to act as if the other order were not there.[26]

The abbot of San Pietro in Ciel d'Oro had been the most important religious figure in Pavia after the bishop; it was impossible to know how the presence of two abbots in San Pietro would affect this, though clearly, the abbot of the Canons was bound to lose some status. The head of the Canons Regular in Pavia could do nothing but obey, in keeping with the spirit of the Augustinian Rule, which makes obedience especially to a superior a matter of fundamental importance. The fateful day of the arrival of the

26. Ibid., 1:13–19 (January 20, 1327). Maiocchi deems the letter of April 1327 from the Commune of Pavia concerning the arrival of the Hermits to be a forgery because Pavia had sided with the emperor and was under papal interdict at this time. This was disputed by Giacinto Romano, "Il codice diplomatico agostiniano di S. Pietro in Ciel d'Oro," *Bollettino della Società pavese di storia patria* 6 (1906), 290–94. A letter of June 1327 from Cardinal Beltrando del Poggetto threatened the Canons with excommunication and an interdict if they did not admit the Augustinian Hermits. See Maiocchi and Casacca, *Codex diplomaticus,* 1: 31–33 (June 19, 1327). It is interesting to compare the Pavian circumstances with situations that arose in post-1648 Germany. The Treaty of Westphalia created a couple of situations in which Protestant and Catholic congregations shared the same ecclesiastical space. See Joachim Whaley, "Religious Toleration in the Holy Roman Empire," in *Toleration in Enlightenment Europe,* ed. Ole Peter Grell and Roy Porter (Cambridge: Cambridge University Press, 2000), 180–82.

Augustinian Hermits was postponed when the forces of the emperor Louis occupied Pavia in 1327. Pope John had excommunicated Louis and subsequently placed Pavia, among other locations, under an interdict; Louis had then supplanted John with a pope of his own choice. In Pavia, Louis seems to have dealt with the Canons Regular and the Augustinian Hermits with equal harshness. The Canons may even have been driven out of the city for a time. In 1331 a truce of sorts was agreed between John and Louis, and the negotiations between the Canons and the Augustinians began in earnest.[27] Guglielmo came to Pavia to supervise them; the first of numerous agreements was reached in June 1331.[28] His intent was to make this new monastery the paragon for his order. Its thirty-five to forty monks vastly outnumbered the five Canons who were there in the early 1330s.

In the middle of the century an Augustinian, Giacomo Bussolari, rallied the Pavians against the Visconti of Milan.[29] On May 27, 1356, the Pavians won a great victory against the Visconti; then the Visconti, in 1359, defeated the count of Monferrato, the ruler of Pavia, and the city surrendered. While Bussolari was exiled, his order was not punished.[30] The Canons were in possession of a generous endowment and were well connected with the families of the local elite. If they had hoped to profit from Bussolari's defeat, the Visconti disappointed them. The Augustinian Hermits remained in their new and imposing cloister and garden on the south side of the cathedral, which they had completed in 1348; their financial needs were answered by many generous donations and alms. At the end of the fourteenth century they commissioned the most prestigious sculpture in the city, the *arca*, which contained scenes of Augustine's life and his

27. At this same time, Opcinus de Canistris paints an idyllic picture of the civic harmony of Pavia in his *Liber de laudibus civitatis ticenensis*. See *Opicino de Canistris, l'anonimo ticinese (Cod. Vaticano palatino lat. 1993)* (Pavia, 1927). He asserts that it was a face-to-face community where everyone knew everybody. Twice a day Pavia's fifty thousand citizens met just to keep in touch. The population, the insignificance of social class, and the participation of the citizens in their governance are overstated.

28. Maiocchi and Casacca, *Codex diplomaticus*, 1:44–50.

29. Giacinto Romano, "Eremitani e canonici regolari in Pavia nel secolo XIV e loro attinenze con la lor cittadina," *Archivio storico lombardo*, ser. 3, vol. 4, year 22 (1895), 5–42. The Canons supported the Visconti and, unlike the Hermits, had close political connections with the Pavian elite.

30. Carlos Alonso, "Bussolari, Giacomo," in *Dizionario biografico degli Italiani* (1980–), 15: 580–82. See also Ugo Mariani, *Il Petrarca e gli agostiniani* (Rome: Edizioni di storia e letteratura, 1946).

subsequent Translations.[31] It was completed sometime between 1360 and 1380. The Canons had to accept that all the monks appearing in the sculpted images of the life and posthumous career of St. Augustine wore the distinctive cowl and habit of the Augustinian Hermits.[32] In these scenes these cowled monks not only attended on Augustine in his life but also received his body in Pavia from Liutprand.

In 1385 the Canons struck back with a long legal brief addressed to Pope Urban VI, which summarized the abuses and injustices committed by the Augustinians. Six years later an investigation was completed that largely supported the Canons' allegations. The Augustinian Hermits then appealed to his successor, Pope Boniface IX.[33] A fistfight broke out when the Hermits entered the church singing psalms while the Canons were singing Vespers. To describe this unseemly situation, a popular saying was invoked: The same household can't keep two dogs. A mediator was appointed to try to resolve their differences. In 1400, Pope Boniface proposed a compromise that resolved in large measure the financial ambiguities created by dual ownership of the cathedral. The division of the cathedral was more firmly laid down: a line was drawn through the middle, with the Canons having the north side, the Augustinians the south. Neither side was allowed unilaterally to change the locks on the parts of the church they shared. But in other matters Rome still seems to have favored the Augustinian Hermits over the Canons.[34]

In 1509 the Canons Regular of the Congregation of Mortara were replaced by those of the Lateran of St. Epiphanius (Lateranesi di S. Epifanio). This alteration provided a new opportunity to reopen the old debate. This time it was restated and clarified that the orders would have primary responsibility for the main altar and crypt altar in alternate months. An attempt was made to allocate fairly all aspects of the hymns and celebrations of the liturgical year. The division of the church on its north-south axis was continued, and a number of disputes about matters of property were

31. The *arca* was probably the accomplishment of Prior Bonifacio Bottigella. See Flavio Fagnani, "Bottigella, Bonifacio," in *Dizionario biografico degli Italiani,* 13:459–60.

32. On this and other related quarrels, see Kaspar Elm, "Augustinus canonicus–Augustinus Eremita," in *Christianity and the Renaissance: Image and Religious Imagination in the Quattrocento,* ed. Timothy Verdon and John Henderson (Syracuse, N.Y.: Syracuse University Press, 1990), 83–107.

33. Maiocchi and Casacca, *Codex diplomaticus,* 1:154–86.

34. Ibid., 1:189–97, 219–25.

also resolved.[35] Needless to say, no formula was devised that could cancel the hard feelings or provide guidelines to handle all subsequent disputes. The brutal politics of the early sixteenth century also affected life at San Pietro. The siege and battle of Pavia in 1527, as well as the numbers of troops quartered in the city in the 1520s, meant that almost no one was safe from the demands of the friendly troops. Pavia's Spanish defenders all but sacked the city while protecting it from the French army outside the walls. In the early 1540s quarrels arose, and again arbitration was sought.[36] Perhaps in an attempt to preempt further quarrels, in 1580, Pope Gregory XIII forbade any search into or moving of St. Augustine's bones.[37] On occasion brawls would erupt between the brotherhoods. Some of the struggles even took place in the cathedral itself: a fight broke out in 1570, and another assault took place in the choir in 1600.[38]

On March 13, 1620, the violence between the two orders resulted in actual bloodshed. San Pietro had been polluted, and again outside arbitrators were sought.[39] In March 1622 a new protocol was drawn up repeating, interpreting, and clarifying the previous agreements. The most recent quarrel had in part had its origin in the bookstand where the massive choir book was placed. The book could be slanted to either side so that the monks could read it from a distance and sing psalms and other prayers. No one was allowed to slam the book shut or otherwise alter its position to impede others from seeing it, and no one was permitted to pass in front of the book or impede the lines of sight of those reading it. Attempts were also made to further define who could say what prayers, when, and on what feast days to prevent the two orders from celebrating religious ceremonies at cross-purposes and thus each frustrating the other. This time a line separating the two religious orders was actually chiseled into the pavement of the cathedral. New incidents nevertheless allowed the quarrel to continue.[40] An ongoing source of aggravation concerned the customary offering made by the officials of the municipality to St. Augustine. In their offi-

35. Ibid., 3:45–55, 57–58, 63–64, 75–76. In 1518 the new order of Canons was allowed to enter San Pietro.

36. Ibid., 3:198–202, 204–8, 210, 212. The next resolution was in 1543.

37. Ibid., 4:74–86.

38. Ibid., 4:13–28, 177–83.

39. Ibid., 4:265–79, 5:1, 8–10.

40. Ibid., 5:8–9.

cial processions to the cathedral, the city's standard was covered by the habit of the Augustinian Hermits. After numerous appeals and counterappeals, a papal commission in 1635 resolved this issue and others.[41] Further restrictions were set down aimed at preventing either Hermits or Canons from disrupting each other's religious services, whether they were held in their chapter houses, the crypt, or the main altar. Also new regulations were made concerning when and which of the cathedral's bells could be rung, and by whom.

Therefore, when on October 1, 1695, workmen hired by the Augustinian Hermits found relics that they claimed were Augustine's, the Canons Regular could not have been expected to rejoice spontaneously at their rivals' good fortune. The discovery of the relics and the miracles associated with them created a situation in which different interpretations and explanations were debated in the presence of a concerned public. What happened in Pavia was not the story of a hostile and repressive investigative process which aimed to educate and rebuke the wayward by intimidation and compulsion. This was frequently what happened when popular religiosity, inspired by miracles associated with sacred images or reports of visions, was not supported by significant clerical support. In Pavia, respected authorities differed, and during the controversy, different interpretations were presented for public perusal. There were two distinct periods of controversy, the first lasting from 1695 to 1704 and the second from 1728 to 1731. The second period was inaugurated by what was essentially a papal declaration of the authenticity of the relics and an order forbidding further dissent. The Invention narrative about Augustine brought out a variety of emotional responses; but despite their differences, they indicate a shared vocabulary and acceptance of premises, and suggest patterns of shared thought and discourse useful in understanding the development of a general reading public in late-seventeenth- and early-eighteenth-century urban areas. They also indicate how elite and popular perceptions of religion might work together to produce their own forms of creative energies, and, they make clear that the elite did not speak with one voice. The controversialists and their publics shared the expectation that historical research could help them understand the inheritance, the rituals, and the beliefs they associated with their patron saint, Augustine.

41. Ibid., 5:19–21, 36–41.

THREE
The Pavian Reading Public and the Controversy about the Bones

THE workmen who discovered Augustine's relics were not members of the general reading public. This, however, does not mean they must have been ignorant of, or indifferent to, the intellectual discourse in other parts of their local community, especially among their clergy. The testimonies collected about the Invention did not probe deeply into their reading knowledge or question their reading habits. They had varying degrees of marginal literacy, and most claimed they could make out the letters written on the marble box that spelled out Augustine's name. Granted their testimony of what they saw did not agree. But they knew what kinds of things they were expected to see. The workers were interviewed at different times and were asked to reproduce by drawing the shapes of the letters exactly as they had seen them. Besides their ability to read and write letters, another bit of testimony recorded was that some of these men knew about different styles of handwriting, and the names the men used for them suggest some awareness of the distinctive characteristics of medieval handwriting. It was not made explicit in the records of their interrogation, but some of the questioners realized that authenticated information about the vanished writing could help date the relics. This was also understood by those who doubted that these were Augustine's relics, for the records include disparaging remarks about those who would accept the statements of manual laborers as if they were experts on matters of palaeography. No manual laborer, the doubters argued, could have anything to say about smudged charcoal writing that could help date the relics. That this issue was raised at all provides telling evidence about the intellectual climate in Pavia. Some knowledge of the revolution in historical study and research brought about by Catholic scholars in the 1680s had reached these workers.

In 1681 the French scholar and historian Jean Mabillon, a Benedictine of the Congregation of St. Maur, born to a family of Norman farmers, published *De re diplomatica* (Concerning diplomatics). This was a technical work that, for the first time, set down a method and principles for dating, criticizing, and determining the authenticity of the documents of the Latin Middle Ages. It is a sign of his achievement that in an academic field that included many of the best minds of the age, his book was recognized for its solutions to specific problems found in manuscript texts, and, more important, as presenting a method for interpreting any medieval Latin manuscript. This work created the science of diplomatics, the critical study of manuscript documents, charters, and letters. Mabillon's book became the textbook of that new science. Recognition of his accomplishment came from both Catholic and Protestant scholars.[1]

Previously, Humanist scholars had developed extremely sophisticated methods for editing the Greek and Latin texts of antiquity. To improve their editing and re-editing, they sought to learn as much as they could about the time when an author composed a text. They studied the languages of antiquity, as well as inscriptions, monuments, and coins. Their endeavor included Greek and Roman authors, pagan and Christian, as well as the textual transmission of the Bible. As they studied the manuscripts of these texts prepared in medieval times, their primary goal was to recover the most likely version of the original ancient text, not to investigate the work habits and traditions of the medieval copyists.[2] Prior to Mabillon's contribution, scholars had attempted the dating of individual items but had not developed a more general theory. Mabillon's interest was in dating and authenticating large numbers of public documents, sacred and secular, concerning property and legal privilege in medieval times.

1. David Knowles, *Great Historical Enterprises* (London: Thomas Nelson and Sons, 1963); Arnaldo Momigliano, "Ancient History and the Antiquarian," in *Studies in Historiography* (New York: Garland Press, 1985), 1–39.

2. The story of this magnificent accomplishment, the creation of modern scholarly methods for the study of the humanities, is a complex one. Something of the range of this revolution in learning is indicated by Robert Weiss, *The Renaissance Discovery of Classical Antiquity* (Oxford: Clarendon Press, 1969); John D'Amico, *Theory and Practice in Renaissance Textual Criticism: Beatus Rhenanus* (Berkeley: University of California Press, 1988); Donald R. Kelley, *The Foundations of Modern Historical Scholarship: Language, Law, and History in the French Renaissance* (New York: Columbia University Press, 1970); Anthony Grafton, *Joseph Scaliger: A Study in the History of Classical Scholarship*, 2 vols. (Oxford: Clarendon Press, 1983–93), and *Commerce with the Classics* (Ann Arbor: University of Michigan Press, 1997); and William McCuaig, *Carlo Sigonio: The Changing World of the Late Renaissance* (Princeton: Princeton University Press, 1989).

In addition to recognizing its obvious historical uses, some intellectuals had great hopes for the future findings to be revealed by this new science.[3] There was an expectation that at long last an impartial observer would be able to discern whether Catholics or Protestants had the better arguments and the more authoritative position about the traditions and patterns of ecclesiastical history. There was also the hope that a definitive text of the Bible might now be established to counter the scandalous approaches of the likes of Spinoza, Hobbes, and La Peyrère.

How these methods of dealing with medieval documents were introduced to the laity or to the men who did the manual labor and other contract work for churches in Pavia is not known. Jean Mabillon had visited Pavia and San Pietro in Ciel d'Oro in early June 1686, and what he had done and where he had prayed had not gone unnoticed or forgotten. The primary purpose of his visit had been to study documents and manuscripts in Pavia's churches.[4] The fact that he had prayed before the crypt altar in San Pietro was remembered and turned into an argument supporting the authenticity of the relics of Augustine. Mabillon found few followers in Italy who were willing to master the rigorous discipline required of his new methods; but this did not preclude an interest in and enthusiasm for the possible results of his new approach. He was known to be generous with his time and willing to demonstrate his method. Mabillon visited the

3. Mabillon's accomplishment was a significant contribution on the side of the Moderns in the famous contemporaneous debate, the Quarrel between the Ancients and the Moderns. Recent scholarship has emphasized the literary and scientific side of the Quarrel, and has given less attention to Mabillon's new science of history. Joseph M. Levine has shown the importance of these new historical methods in *The Battle of the Books: History and Literature in the Augustan Age* (Ithaca: Cornell University Press, 1991). For an assessment of Mabillon's accomplishment in the context of the ambitions of the French cultural world of Louis XIV, see Françoise Waquet, *Le modèle français et l'Italie savante: conscience de soi et perception de l'autre dans la République des letters (1660–1750)* (Rome: École Française de Rome, Palais Farnèse, 1989), 299–332.

4. In the library of San Pietro, Mabillon found a document dated 712 that indicated Augustine's relics were already in Pavia and had arrived perhaps as early as 710. He published the document in his report of his Italian journey. See Jean Mabillon and Michel Germain, *Musaeum Italicum seu collectio veterum scriptorum ex bibliothecis italicis,* 2 vols. (Paris: Jean Boudot, 1687), 1:218–22. In 1956 these documents were shown to be forgeries. See Beniamino Pagnin, "Falsi diplomi reali ed imperiali per S. Pietro in Ciel d'Oro di Pavia nel secolo VIII al XII," *Bollettino della Società pavese di storia patria,* n.s. 8 (1956), 15–42. For Mabillon as a teacher of the Italians, see Arnaldo Momigliano, "Mabillon's Italian Disciples," in *Essays in Historiography* (Oxford: Blackwell, 1977), 271–93.

Hermits' library and may well have pointed out some aspects of a manuscript that demonstrated its date of composition. His demonstration could have been repeated by someone present, who might have shown sufficient expertise and use of technical language to impress members of the laity. The audience would have come away with a new respect for the age and venerability of the objects being preserved in their local monastery.

Although a few of the workmen conveyed in their testimony that they had knowledge of different types of medieval handwriting, they were not asked how they acquired this knowledge. It must have been obvious or else seemed unproblematic to the investigators. Colli, who conducted the questioning, had had training as an Inquisitor. The workers' familiarity with these matters did not disturb him. Their evidence about the writing on the box had credibility because it echoed the jargon associated with Mabillon's new science. The mere memory of seeing writing or letters was not enough, however; some description of their shape and orthography was needed to provide convincing corroborative detail. The declaration that some of the letters that spelled "Augustinus" were "Gothic" made their testimony more believable. The vocabulary that the stoneworkers and artists who found the box used to describe this potential historical evidence came close enough to the preconceptions of some intellectuals to persuade them of its truth. By the same token, they antagonized other scholars, who sought to discredit their testimony by ad hominem attacks. "Gothic" may well have had a fairly precise meaning to the clergy; to the workers it may simply have been synonymous with "old." No one argued with the identification of Lombard crosses on the lead box that contained the relics. The crosses gave circumstantial support to the date of the relics but could reveal nothing about the identity of the bones. What the workmen knew about crosses or styles of medieval art was not investigated. The workers, it would seem, had not just entered into the mythic time of the saint's legend; they were also participants in a complicated and confusing turning point in the history of historical research.

The Invention of Augustine, which in the tradition of this sort of narrative should have resulted in the restoration of the saint to an unchanging eternal presence in his community, had the effect of emphasizing Augustine's historical situation and the relics' presence in historical time. With the Invention of St. Mark, it is difficult to distinguish the stage management of the Doge from the supposedly spontaneous discovery of the relics, let alone other motives such as the eagerness of the people to come together in their universal approbation of their saint, their rulers, and the power of the Venetian state. In Pavia it is hard to imagine any stage management. Instead of a spontaneous display of unity, Pavia's divided cathedral produced a public disputation between members of the clergy addressed to the lay congregation. The case of St. Mark operated on the level of symbolism, affirming a truth about Venice in a nondiscursive sort of thinking, represented in a mosaic. What happened in Pavia has elements of this experience, but it primarily involved critical analysis of the historical evidence and interpretations of cultural traditions contained in medieval documents. The controversy was represented in the printed word, most often in a polemic addressed to the general reading public. Instead of an attempt to impose one view dogmatically, there was a debate—a free one, at least within certain constraints. No one argued that all relics were frauds, or even that these specific ones were. All parties agreed that a sacred burial site had been found; the question was whose burial place it was.

The first published account of the Invention was a pamphlet written by Romualdo Ghisoni describing the discovery of the bones. Ghisoni was a member of an Augustinian order, the Barefoot Hermits, or Scalzi; his order was located at San Carlo, not San Pietro. His account was published sometime in 1696, in Latin, titled *De inventione corporis S. Patris Augustini* (Concerning the Invention of the body of our Holy Father St. Augustine). The work was promptly translated into Italian by his colleague Padre Mathis as *Dell'inventione del sacro corpo di S. Agostino.* It was published as a pamphlet, of quarto format, consisting of eight unnumbered pages, by "the heirs" of Carlo Magri's printing house—probably his son or sons.[5] The pamphlet included a woodcut image of the silver casket with its decoration of Lombard crosses. The text described the circumstances of the Invention, the different boxes, and the contents. Ghisoni was fairly certain that the wooden fragments found with the bones were bits of the marvelous log that Augustine had used to augment those main beams that

5. Mathis da Carmagnuola, *Dell'invenzione del sacro corpo di S. Agostino nel primo d'ottobre 1695* (Pavia: Eredi Carlo Magri). This is the same as BNPav Mss. Ticinensis 32.9. In France and in Germany the widow of a publisher would frequently assume his role, sometimes using her widowed status to advertise the shop for years after her husband's death. In Italy, after the death of a printer, the title page would attribute the work to the printer's unnamed *eredi,* or male heirs.

had been cut too short when he supervised the construction of churches in Africa.

As with most books published at this time, there are few records telling how many were printed and what people paid for them. We know even less about the numbers and the sale prices of printed pamphlets and broadsides. In terms of books, a print run of more than 1,500 copies in one edition would have been unusual, while a print run of fewer than 400 copies would have been on the low side for this period.[6] We do know that the print run for one long book in the subsequent controversy on the authenticity of the bones, Giuseppe Beretti's *Lynchnus,* was 300 copies: the Hermits paid the costs of the printing.[7] Ghisoni's magnum opus might well have been in the same range, but these figures are not reliable guides for the size of editions of Latin or Italian pamphlets. (The range for many modern scholarly books is 500 to 1,500 copies.)

The market for most of a printer's productions in early modern Europe was the local community, especially for ephemeral works like pamphlets. But even cheap works printed for local buyers required marketing in order that they be sold. Typically, in continental Europe in the 1690s, printed items required some sort of permission and registration with representatives of the state and often with those of the clergy as well. In Italy these took the form of approval letters, which certified the orthodoxy of the work's contents. These letters—and, more important, who authored them—were part of the publisher's or author's marketing strategy. The content of these letters was usually pro forma and revealed little about a book's content. What was significant from the perspective of sales was not what the letter said but who said it. The reputations of these individuals advertised an item and identified it as a work of genuine interest in much the same way as the blurbs of praise that decorate the dust jackets and covers of modern books. The idea was to choose someone as an approver who would have a clear identity to potential book buyers so as to persuade them to make the purchase. A dedication could be expected to have a similar effect. The person to whom the book was dedicated might well be its financial patron. The recipients of most dedicatory letters were members of the elite,

6. For a near-contemporary accounting of the costs of a major publication in Venice of Coronelli's *Biblioteca,* see the Biblioteca Marciana di Venezia Mss. Misc. 2168.

7. Rodolfo Maiocchi and Nazereno Casacca, *Codex diplomaticus Ord. E.S. Augustini Papiae* (Pavia: C. Rossetti, 1905–15), 5:129.

secular or clerical, while approval letters tended to be written by non-nobles who had a personal connection with an author.

The Latin edition and the Italian translation of Ghisoni's pamphlet offer an example of how this system operated.[8] Ghisoni wrote the Latin text, his friend Padre Mathis translated it, and Michele Colli, who was investigating the bones' authenticity, provided the approval letter. Ghisoni was an old man in 1695. In May of that year he had completed in manuscript a book titled *Flavia Papia sacra,* a history of Pavia's religious communities, saints, and relics. His *De inventione* in fact consisted of several pages from the first part of the *Flavia,* which he updated with the news of the Invention. The *Flavia* was to be his masterpiece and would enshrine his reputation as a master of Pavia's ecclesiastical history, but the book was not yet published at the time of the Invention.

Ghisoni's work was in the tradition of the great antiquaries of the previous century who had written on the customs and rituals of their community. These books, while organized according to certain principles and categories, read more like a miscellany than a history. Some of what these books preserved were oral traditions, and on occasion examples of what we would call popular culture. Most of the oral traditions involved the memories of the local clerical elite and the popular traditions of the educated. Such antiquarian compilations first appeared in the early days of printing. Giacomo Gualla was the most illustrious of the scholars who first sought to document the religious treasures and customs of Pavia in print. His *Sanctuarium Papiae* was published in Pavia in 1505 and again in 1587. It contained an account of the churches and relics in Pavia: hundreds of relics were listed, among them relics of Job and Tobias as well as a nipple of Mary Magdalene, which he described as impressive ("integra & valde"). Gualla's method had been followed by Bernardo Sacco in his *De italicarum rerum varietate et elegantia* of 1587; his work focused on Pavian secular history. The Canons Regular had their own local historian, Agostino Ticinensis, who in 1500 published *De situ orbis.* At the end of the century, in 1597, Spelta published a history of Pavia's bishops in Italian, and Stefano Breventano published a vernacular account of Pavia's aristocracy in his 1570 *Historia delle antichità, nobilità, et delle cose notabili . . . di Pavia.*

8. For a description of this system in operation in the Naples of this time, see Harold Stone, *Vico's Cultural History: The Production and Transmission of Ideas in Naples, 1685–1750* (Leiden: E. J. Brill, 1997), 17–19.

Ghisoni brought Gualla up-to-date, noting, for example, that in 1667, San Pietro received as a bequest from the empress Margaret the breast of Mary Magdalene. Ghisoni divided his work in four parts: the first part concerned the individual saints of Pavia, focusing on the churches in which they were buried; the second concerned the careers of these saints; the third described their relics; and the fourth recorded the generous benefactions made to ecclesiastical institutions from the time of the Lombards up to the present.

The method followed in such works was to prepare extracts from all the sources available that mentioned the city, its sacred structures, and local worthies. These would include references taken from works such as Vincent of Beauvais's *Speculum quadruplex: sive Speculum maius*, a fourteenth-century universal history, and Jacobus de Voragine's *Legenda aurea*, a compendium of saints' lives that had made mention of Pavia. Bede the Venerable and William of Malmesbury, though historians of England, wrote of events in Pavia and would also have been among the sources. An important document for Ghisoni was an early-fourteenth-century manuscript describing Pavia, the *Anonymi ticinensis liber de laudibus civitatis ticinensis* (The book concerning the praiseworthy things of the city of Pavia by an anonymous Pavian). The work was written for the papal court in Avignon, but nothing is known about the author, who is presumed to have been a cleric-courtier from Pavia working in Avignon. For reasons that are now unknown, Ghisoni identified the author as "Sigisbert"; but no more is known of "Sigisbert" than of the anonymous Pavian. Probably no one would have noticed this except that, because of the discovery of the bones, Ghisoni's book became the crib for most authors seeking a quick tour of the relevant primary sources. Poor Ghisoni was ridiculed by some readers, who joked about the baptizing and rebaptizing of the poor chronicler from Anonymous to Sigisbert. It is possible that Ghisoni had access to a manuscript that is no longer available, but he may also have made a mistake confusing the author of the *De laudibus* with that of the *Cronica* of Sigebertus Gemblacense (Sigebert of Gembloux).[9] Ghisoni also needed to study up on authors such as Petrarch who had stayed in Pavia and visited

9. This is the hypothesis put forth by Rodolfo Maiocchi and Ferruccio Quintavalle in their edition of *Anonymi ticinensis, liber de laudibus civitatis ticinensis*, in *Rerum italicarum scriptores: raccolta degli storici italiani*, vol. 11, pt. 1 (Città di Castello: S. Lapi, 1903), xvi–xxix. Sigebert of Gembloux, *Chronica*, ed. L. C. Bethmann (Hanover: Weidmann, 1844), can be found in *Monumenta Germaniae historica*, vol. 6, *Scriptores*.

San Pietro. Petrarch became an authority in the controversy because one of his letters spoke of Augustine's having been buried in a dark and secret place. Ghisoni was expected to keep up-to-date on modern Pavian authors who had written about their city; he even needed to study unpublished manuscripts to make his work complete. He consulted the "Libro Rosso" (The red book), a manuscript, dated 1600, written by a Canon Regular, Giovanni Imperatore. Imperatore too spoke of Augustine's bones as being buried in a dark and secret place and included other information not found in earlier accounts. From this motley of evidence, Ghisoni assembled his account of the saints and sacred spaces of Pavia.

Ghisoni's pamphlet on Augustine's relics took the relevant parts from his unpublished work and reviewed all that was known about the two Translations of Augustine. The dates of both Translations, he noted, remained a matter of controversy. The disputes for or against various dates involved the most respected ecclesiastical historians of the seventeenth and eighteenth centuries. Baronio had dated Augustine's move to Sardinia in 504; contemporaneously with Ghisoni, Tillemont, a Jansenist and a historian of late antiquity, argued for 496. Early in the eighteenth century, a French Augustinian, Guillaume Bonjour, argued for 508, but his contribution was largely unknown because it was not published until the early twentieth century.[10] All that was known about this Translation was that it had occurred; with the second Translation from Sardinia to Pavia, there was at least one contemporary, Bede, who recorded that it had happened, though he was geographically remote from the event. Bede's *Chronica* placed the second Translation in 725; Baronio also believed it to be in 725.[11] The historian of the Canons Regular, Gabriel Pennotto, rely-

10. Guillaume Bonjour, *Analecta Augustiniana* 2 (1907–8), 442–96, dated the second Translation to Pavia between 718 and 726. He also investigated the Translation of Augustine's arm to England for King Canute, which I will discuss later. See Guillaume Bonjour, "De brachio Sancti Patris Augustini Coventreiam translato," *Analecta Augustiniana* 3 (1909–10), 366–87. Benedikt Hackett, "San Pietro in Ciel d'oro, Pavia," in *Augustine in Iconography History and Legend,* ed. Joseph C. Schnaubelt and Frederick Van Fleteren (New York: Peter Lang, 1999), 200, 213–15, describes Bonjour's contribution to the controversy. Bonjour's analysis remained in manuscript until it was published in the second volume (1907–8) of the *Analecta Augustiniana.* Hackett notes Bonjour also wrote on the Translation of Augustine's arm to Coventry in England, which I will discuss later. This account was first published in the third volume of the same issue.

11. Bede, *Chronica de sex huius saeculi aetatibus,* ed. Theodor Mommsen, 3 vols. (Berlin: Weidmann, 1892–98), 3:223–354 . Some have cautioned against regarding Bede's date as too

ing in part on a Pavian inscription, concluded it was in 721. Beretti's *Lynchnus* (written after Ghisoni's death) refuted this date by showing that the inscription was in fact modern. Mabillon argued for 712; Antoine Pagi, the great commentator and critic of Baronio, preferred 722. Proposed dates ranged from 709 to 734; as Muratori prudently summarized the issue in the middle of the eighteenth century, the actual date was uncertain, but the fact of the Translation was most certain.[12] Ghisoni's work was one of the lesser contributions to the project of dating the events of the early Middle Ages; getting the dates right was one of the primary tasks in Ghisoni's kind of antiquarian research.

Ghisoni accepted the convention that authors of vast antiquarian knowledge wrote their works in Latin. For him, it was a mark of their authority and erudition. One presumes that, among those who counted, Ghisoni's project was well known for many years and the final product expected with eagerness. But this could not have been a large number of people. Ghisoni wrote his pamphlet on the Invention of Augustine in Latin because in his view that was the language in which an author of his profile and reputation, or potential reputation, wrote. Now, there were advantages in having an account of the Invention published in Latin by Pavia's foremost ecclesiastical historian, but publicity was not one of them. The intended audience for such a piece could not be relied on to purchase a work in Latin by an unknown author. Most of these people probably would not have known of Ghisoni, his reputation, or of his soon-to-be-printed great work. Therefore, while there were legal requirements for an approval letter, it made good marketing sense to associate the pamphlet with Michele Colli, whose name had been connected with the Augustine Invention from the beginning. The purpose of the pamphlet was not to announce the Invention, for that news had spread with the event itself. The appearance of the pamphlet months after the event suggests that an attempt was

exact. Cesare Baronio, *Annales ecclesiastici,* 37 vols. (Paris: Berri-Ducis, 1864–83), annus 725, published a letter, whose author is now referred to as "Pseudo-Oldradus," which gave support to 710. Baronio, however, argued for Bede's 725. On Baronio, see Cyriac K. Pullapilly, *Caesar Baronius: Counter-Reformation Historian* (Notre Dame, Ind.: University of Notre Dame Press, 1975).

12. Jan T. Hallenbeck, *The Transferal of the Relics of St. Augustine of Hippo from Sardinia to Pavia in the Early Middle Ages* (Lewiston, N.Y.: Edwin Mellen Press, 1988), 113–29, summarizes all the arguments, grants the uncertainty, but believes that the best argument can be made for 723–24 or 724–25 (128).

being made to stonewall recognition of the authenticity of the relics. By bringing in Ghisoni, the Hermits may have hoped that the Canons would concede to his erudition, but that did not happen.

I noted earlier that Ghisoni's *Flavia Papia sacra* had received its approval letters in 1695, but it was not published until 1699, again, as with the pamphlet, by the heirs of Carlo Magri. It appeared more than a year after Ghisoni's death, which occurred on November 13, 1697. Mathis apparently saw the work through its printing and prepared the index. We do not know whether the four-year delay resulted from the ill health of the author, the desire for a posthumous publication, the complexity of the venture, or the lack of financial resources. Paper was the most expensive commodity in the preparation of a book. It is also a genuine possibility that Ghisoni could not find a publisher for a work of erudition. Another Pavian, Antonio Gatti, despairing of finding a publisher for his *De antiquitate urbis ticinensis* (Concerning the ancient ways of Pavia), simply burned his entire manuscript in the early eighteenth century.[13] In any event, Ghisoni's book provided the essential guide to the primary source material for the controversy that arose about the identity of the bones.

Going into print was not the only option available to those involved in local scholarly controversies at this time. For certain types of controversies, the circulation of a manuscript was the medium of choice.[14] On the face of it, given that the number of monks in the two orders sharing San Pietro was around thirty, a manuscript controversy would have been appropriate for such an audience. But perhaps even from the beginning, it was clear that the interested audience included members of other religious orders and a substantial lay readership as well. We do know that sometime in 1696, Ferdinando Leva, one of the Canons Regular at San Pietro's, began writing a manuscript attacking the claim that the bones were those of Au-

13. *Giornale dei letterati d'Italia* 4 (1710), 251–52. Similar problems faced antiquarians in other regions. The case of Bristol later in the century is described by Jonathan Bary, "Provincial Town Culture, 1640–1780: Urbane or Civic?" in *Interpretation and Cultural History,* ed. Joan Pittock and Andrew Wear (London: Macmillan, 1991), 198–234, esp. 211–15.

14. In England, scribal publication was a minor industry. See Harold Love, *Scribal Publication in Seventeenth-Century England* (Oxford: Clarendon Press, 1993). During this same period in Naples, there was a productive tension between book and manuscript publication. For a description, see Stone, *Vico's Cultural History,* 34–45, 51–64.

gustine. He asserted that Colli had been hired by the Augustinian Hermits to discredit the Canons and to take their saint away from them. According to Leva, the Canons had had the bones of St. Augustine in their care since they had been entrusted with them by the Lombard king Liutprand. The Hermits had only arrived on the scene much later and had no proper claim or title to, or authentic information about, the location of the bones. Leva feigned surprise at Colli's ignorance of the early history of the church of San Pietro. He turned his attention to an unnamed work, perhaps Ghisoni's *De inventione,* which was written, he says, by a "brainless" Hermit. The whole purpose of this Hermit's work had been to discredit the role of the Canons in the Translation of Augustine and their subsequent activities in Pavia. Here the argument breaks off, as Leva explains in the text itself, because he was seriously ill with a high fever. While he was sick, Leva goes on, St. Augustine appeared to him in a dream-vision (Leva insists it was a vision, not a dream) and told him to stop writing against the work of Colli. And that is what he did: Leva dates the end of the manuscript April 8, 1697.[15]

Later that year at a meeting of the Accademia degli Affidati (Academy of the Trusty Ones) held on the eve of St. Augustine's feast day, August 27, Leva presented a number of poems about St. Augustine. The fourth in this sonnet sequence describes what happened to him on February 19 of that year, when Augustine appeared to him and told him to stop attacking Colli.[16] It is impossible to know if he had prepared his manuscript attack on Colli with publication in mind, nor do we know how far what he did complete circulated. The copy that survives is clearly not a working draft but was prepared for the use of the Augustinian Hermits. What had happened to Leva was the subject of gossip in Pavia, but the diffusion of the story could just as easily have come from word of mouth as from those who heard his sonnet sequence on Augustine or read the original manuscript or a copy. In the Italian cultural world of the late seventeenth century, academies like the Affidati gave prestige to individual participants and linked intellectuals to local patronage networks. The primary purpose

15. BNPav Mss. Ticinensis 22.10, "In nomine Jesu christu," 11 unnumbered leaves, presented in Bellelli's *In causa identitatis* (*Collectio actorum,* 1:4), under the title "Responsio apologetica P.P. Hermanitanos." See also BNPav Mss. Ticinensis 234, "Memorie e pareri," "Ad adm RRPP Eremitanos Responsia apologetica."

16. BNPav Mss. Ticinensis 32. The sonnets and Leva's manuscript were prepared for some sort of circulation by the Augustinian Hermit Martire Belgradi.

of most of these academies was not to present new knowledge but to affirm the bond between poetry or fine writing and its patrons, the aristocratic elite. The poems presented before the academy were probably intended for the audience at the meeting alone, though they may have circulated in manuscript.[17] Publication was not necessary to affirm the accomplishment of the poet; no other peer review process beyond recitation was required to confirm Leva's standing in Pavia. Frequently this kind of publicity was all that an author sought or needed for the advancement of his career or confirmation of his position in the local scene. In any event, Leva's story was well known in Pavia, and in the documents prepared to authenticate the relics in 1728, it was used as a sort of corroborating evidence. While it is clear that his dream-vision experience had a profound effect on him, it does not seem to have altered the views of his fellow Canons.

Leva's manuscript is the only written evidence of early opposition to the authenticity of the relics. All we know is that despite popular enthusiasm for the Invention, no official approval was forthcoming. In 1698, Bernard de Montfauçon, a French aristocrat, a Benedictine from St. Maur, and a student of Mabillon, arrived in Pavia to examine its antiquities and its manuscripts. He was a man of phenomenal energy and capacious memory who, in 1708, was to create a scientific method for the study of Greek manuscripts that paralleled what Mabillon had provided for medieval Latin. After a journey on long and dusty roads, he arrived in Pavia on July 22, 1698. The War of the League of Augsburg, or the Nine Years' War, was still going on. This made it impossible for Montfauçon to visit Turin and see the famous shroud, since a French army of Louis XIV was attacking Piedmont.

Montfauçon summarized the controversy as it stood when he arrived: Augustine's first Translation had occurred in 504, the second in 721 or 725; though there was some dispute about the exact year, the Translations were accepted as certain. Attempts seem to have been made to involve him in the controversy in Pavia while he was there, but he avoided publicly committing himself. When in Pavia he looked at the Brescian Chronicle and

17. Jane O. Newman describes the significance and conventions of this kind of poetry in *Pastoral Conventions: Poetry, Language, and Thought in Seventeenth-Century Nuremberg* (Baltimore: Johns Hopkins University Press, 1990). In 1735 the Accademia degli Oziosi of Naples published a volume of occasional verse honoring St. Augustine. Although Padua is identified as the place of publication, its origin was probably Naples. See *Vari componimenti* (Padua, 1735). Giambattista Vico and Paolo Mattia Doria were among the contributors.

was shown the Chapel of St. Aphian, where some said Augustine's body had been moved in 1223. One view held that the body had been in the Canons' monastery of Mortara; others said the real location was St. Mostiola, the former residence of the Augustinian Hermits. Montfauçon knew about the Gothic letters supposedly seen by the workers, and he listened to the accounts of the exhumations. Given what was said about the moldered condition of the bones, he did not see how any reliable conclusions could be based on such evidence. The well behind the altar that Pope Leo X had compared to Augustine's inexhaustible wisdom contained, according to Montfauçon, just about enough water to nourish a couple of plants. His 1702 account of his travels, the *Diarium italicum,* was studiously noncommittal but guardedly skeptical about the chance of these bones' belonging to Augustine. In such matters, a wait-and-see attitude was essentially the same as a negative judgment.

In 1696, 1697, 1698, and 1699, Colli presented the case for the bones and attempted to force a decision in their favor. He did this with a mixture of official reports in Latin and more popular summaries, which he published in Italian. In 1696 he published what he called a *Summarium*; it was the first part of a publication issued under the uniform title *Identitatis reliquiarum corporis S. Augustini Episcopi & ecclesiae doctoris in templo S. Pietro in Caeolo Aureo Papiae nuper casu inventarum die prima Novembris, 1695* (The identity of relics of the body of St. Augustine, Bishop, father of the Church, recently found by chance in the Cathedral of San Pietro in Ciel d'Oro, Pavia, on November 1, 1695). In the next part, published in 1696 or 1697, called *Iuris,* Colli noted the mistake made in the title about the date of the Invention: it should have been October, not November. The *Summarium* consisted of twenty unnumbered pages and contained two illustrations. One was an image of Augustine and his casket with his name ("Augustinus") written on the side; the other was of a memorial altar erected in honor of Giuseppe Crippa, the recently deceased prior of the Augustinian Hermits. This juxtaposition of Augustine's grave and Crippa's memorial indicated the strong continuity felt by members of the Augustinian Hermits between themselves and their patron and spiritual founder. Colli described how the relics were found, their location, and the two official visitations, and included the reports of the anatomists. Then Colli turned to the written documentation that supported his assertion that these were

Augustine's bones. He cited all of the papal bulls written about San Pietro that made mention of the relics of St. Augustine, taking particular note of any references to their location. His aim was to prove the continuous presence of Augustine's relics in San Pietro, and the awareness of the most respected religious authority, the pope, of where they were.

Colli dealt with some of the troubling aspects of the traditions concerning St. Augustine's relics, for example, the stories about two Canons named Basil and Florentius who were said to have hidden Augustine's body. Nothing was known of them except their forenames, and actually there was confusion about these too. They were either two Canons—if they were Canons—named Basil and Florentius, or one person named Basil of Florence (Basilio da Fiorenza). Colli concerned himself only with the standard story that they were two Canons. At some time in the remote past, fearing that San Pietro's was about to be looted, Basil and Florentius took it upon themselves to move Augustine's relics to a safe and very secret place, "in fundo confessori." It was a location that they knew about, and perhaps had passed on to other Canons. One document suggested that the Chapel of St. Aphian was the temporary location, but when, if ever, the body had been moved back was not made clear. The chronicles that recorded the story gave no indication when this supposed Translation took place. Some thought it happened in the time of Charlemagne's invasion of Italy in 774; the dates 1263 and 1327 had supporters as well. Colli accepted that a temporary Translation had occurred, but from all the other evidence it was clear to him that the relics were subsequently returned to their proper place. From his point of view this supposed third Translation of Augustine's body created no problems because the rest of the historical record was so rich in testimonies about the bones' location.

Another piece of the historical record that Colli presented as decisive concerned the purchase by King Canute of England of Augustine's arm. Canute himself did not negotiate the deal; it was not even all that clear that the relics were actually purchased under his auspices. The evidence for this transaction came from William of Malmesbury, who wrote about one hundred years after the event. In fact, William describes the event twice, once in his *De gestis regum anglorum* and again in *De gestis pontificum anglorum.* According to him, the archbishop of Canterbury, whom he calls Ethelnot in the first book and then Egelnod in the second, purchased St. Augustine's left arm for one hundred talents of silver and one talent of gold. The relic found its place in the Coventry Cathedral; later it was destroyed during the Reformation in 1539. Colli had not in fact descended to the primary source. He may have gone no further than Ghisoni's manuscript, but he probably relied on Cesare Baronio's *Annales ecclesiastici,* published in the early seventeenth century. Baronio had dated the sale to 1027 and had assigned it to King Canute (1022 is now the accepted date for the Synod of Pavia and the most likely occasion for the transaction). What interested Colli in all of this was the anatomists' list of the bones found in the box. Although they included a right radius and ulna, there were no bones from the left forearm. While not proof positive, Colli regarded this absence as significant evidence. In addition, Augustine's heart was supposed to be in Antwerp, or some thought Brussels, and nothing found in Pavia could dispute this. Ragusa (Dubrovnik) since the fourteenth century had possessed Augustine's axial vertebrae, and a finger was in Parma, and these also were not found among the bones enumerated by the doctors: much of the backbone and the bones of the hands were missing.

Colli's *Summarium* was later translated into Italian and it was also used as part of the introductory material in the 1729 *Collectio actorum.*[18] After the *Summarium,* Colli issued *Iuris.* Each of these was part of the full case he was expected to present. Colli must have had to listen to an earful of complaints about his investigation, either directly or indirectly. The different publications appear, in part, to be addressing or confronting unnamed opponents. There is much repetition of argument and description in these pamphlets; each, though, is distinguished by a shift in emphasis, which can be read as a response to particular criticisms, questions, or arguments. His answers seem designed to counter attacks or solidify the convictions of his supporters on specific issues raised by contrary interpretations of the historical evidence. He repeats the same argument with different emphases in these publications. In *Iuris,* consisting of fourteen unnumbered pages, he explained how, according to the Council of Trent, relics ought to be verified. It was recognized that sometimes it was impossible to have absolute proof. The Council of Trent had acknowledged that there were what it called moral certainties about relics, which were deduced by means of probable reason, and these should have a recognized standing as well. This, according to Colli, was the kind of evidence that ought to be accepted here. By consensus it was agreed that Augustine was buried in the

18. Fulgenzio Bellelli, *Collectio actorum* (1729), 1:41–97. It is the first item in the Biblioteca Marciana di Venezia manuscript Mss. Clas. V cod. LVIII (5820).

crypt altar. One body alone had been found in that crypt, and therefore it made sense to conclude that it was indeed Augustine's. No other body was expected to be found in the crypt, and the discovery supported the continuous presumption that Augustine's body was buried there.

Furthermore, Colli argued, the complex deals worked out by the papacy with the two orders about sharing the church, and particularly the crypt altar, would not make any sense unless Augustine's relics were in fact there. In 1580, Colli noted, Pope Gregory XIII expressly forbade either the Canons or the Hermits to do anything with Augustine's body. Presumably the pope was talking about some tangible object, for if no one knew where the body was, what argument or eventuality was this agreement supposed to preclude? The tradition, therefore, that in 1632 (or perhaps 1627, according to another source) a Canon named Glicerio Landriano engaged in a nocturnal excavation of Augustine's remains had to be false. Such a man would not openly defy the papacy, Colli asserted. The Canons solved this problem simply by redating Glicerio's discovery of the saint's body to 1579 and then repeated the same argument. The Canons' conclusion was that if Basil and Florentius had not hidden the body, then certainly Glicerio had done so.

Later Colli issued a *Juris allegationes,* consisting of eight unnumbered pages, in which he repeated much of what he had previously argued, though this time we learn that according to some records, 133 bodies were buried in San Pietro. Another official visitation was held with the abbots and bishop on March 15, 1698, but again, nothing definitive was concluded. This apparently was too much for Giulio Baudini, an Augustinian Hermit of Pavia. On April 15 he published a small book of forty-one pages titled *Tumulus S.P. Augustini, magni ecclesiae magistri, ac augustissimi ticini regii protectoris dissertatione historico-canonica* (The tomb of our Holy Father Augustine, teacher of the Church, most august protector of Pavia: a historical-canonical essay). It was published in Pavia by Giacomo Andrea Ghidini.

Baudini's argument covers much the same ground as had Colli. His account starts with Liutprand and goes through the whole history of the relics. By page twenty-two he can no longer restrain his irony, and charges that his unnamed opponents seem to expect proofs to follow the form and have the certainty of Aristotle's logic. His work was later attacked for what were called its gross historical and theological errors: in a passing remark about the heresies of Wycliffe and the Waldensians, he misidentified one of their greatest persecutors as a proponent of these heresies. Baudini concludes with a defense of the miracles that had recently occurred in Pavia. These had apparently come under serious question, and Baudini attempts to show that nothing diabolic or demonic was involved in any of the cures. He concludes with an account of Countess Gambarana's sick child.

Twelve days later, in conjunction with or perhaps spurred on by Baudini, Colli issued another section of his *Identitatis,* this one called *Discursus.* Dated April 27, 1698, it is twenty-eight pages long and was also published by Ghidini in Pavia. In it he summarizes what had been published, discusses the miracles associated with the Invention, and this time takes the historical argument back to the Sardinian Translation and brings his account right up to the visitation of the relics on March 15, 1698. He again deals with the issue of the Brescian Chronicle and the story about Basil and Florentius. His conclusion is more straightforward and bolder than before: relics greeted with such proofs should be worshipped and revered, he declares. In August of this same year he published another pamphlet with the Latin title *Summarium ex depositionibus testium productorum in causa identitatis in causa identitatis Sac. ossium D. Augustini noviter inventorum* (Summary taken from the deposition of witnesses brought forth on the matter of the identity of the recently found bones of St. Augustine). Despite the title, the text is in Italian. It is much more personal in tone. Colli tells us that he is now seventy-five, and that since he was twelve years old, he had always believed that St. Augustine's bones were buried in the crypt altar. He recounts the five miracles that had been performed, writing with a renewed intensity and wonder at the evident blessings shown to Pavia and to San Pietro's after the recovery of the bones. He suggests that there were many more cures than those recorded here, but he does not add any specifics.

Later that year Colli published a pamphlet of twenty-eight unnumbered pages titled *Ex depositionibus testium examinatorum, rationes, et iura in causa identitatis Sac. Ossium D. Augustini noviter inventorum in eccles. S. Petri in Caelo aureo Papiae* (Taken from the testimonies of witness, the arguments and the legal rights concerning the case of the identity of the bones of Divine Augustine recently found in the church of San Pietro in Ciel d'Oro in Pavia). He again takes up the issue of when the supposed Translation performed by Basil and Florentius took place. One presumes that Colli was continuing to hear complaints from supporters of the Canons Regulars. This time he admits that, yes, errors had been made in the inventory of the bones, but they were typographical errors, not those of the anatomists. And he records with obvious pleasure the news of another great discovery, the finding of the bones of the apostle Bartholomew in Benevento.

On February 17, 1699, there was another meeting of the leaders of the Canons and the Hermits, where Colli tried to show that, given that everyone accepted as correct what the historian Gualla had written in the early sixteenth century, therefore both sides could not be far from agreement. But perhaps San Pietro's tradition of discord precluded consensus. When no conclusion was reached, Colli decided to pursue the matter to the next step. He then wrote a *Responsio novis motivis fisci, cum productione omnium jurium, spectantium ad identitatem ven. ossium S. Augustini, noviter inventorum* (Response with new rigorously argued reasons, with the profession of all the legal claims concerning the venerable bones of St. Augustine, recently found). Once again he reviewed all the salient features of the Invention and the documentary evidence showing that the crypt altar was Augustine's burial place.

Around the same time, March 7, 1699, he published a *Compendium totius processus, constructi in causem identitatis, Sacrorum ossium S. Augustini Episcopi* . . . (A compendium of the case built up concerning the identity of the sacred bones of St. Augustine, bishop . . .). This work was supplemented by the numerous testimonials of supporters of his conclusions; it was like a publication of a collection of approval letters. He solicited ecclesiastics to write up statements of support. These were given the uniform title of *votum*. These voices of support were also published separately, or at least some were, and they were gathered together by Colli and Nicolo Rubini and issued under the title *Vota clarissimorum & insignium theologorum in causa identititatis sacr. ossium S.P. Augustini ecclesiae doctoris eximii* (Votes of the most illustrious and renowned churchmen on the case of the identity of the sacred bones of the outstanding doctor of the Church, our Holy Father Augustine). Twenty-six churchmen went on record supporting the claim that these were St. Augustine's bones. Their approval, of course, was contingent on the evidence being exactly as Colli described it. In February 1699 rumors reached Ludovico Muratori, who was still in Milan, about a work in preparation concerning the authenticity of the bones. But the reference is too vague to determine whether he was referring to Colli's publications; perhaps the talk was about Giovanni Beretti's massive book, which appeared the following year.[19] In 1700 the head of the Augustinian Hermits, Antonio Pacini, spent four months in Pavia and attempted to resolve the disputed issues, but to no avail.

I estimate that some 3,000 and perhaps as many as 8,000 copies of the ten pamphlets written by Colli, Mathis, and Baudini were printed and in circulation in the Pavia area. If each *votum* was printed, and even presuming only 100 to be printed of each, that would mean over 2,500 more items were circulating in Pavia.[20] This number of items indicates that a remarkable amount of printed matter entered booksellers' shops or was distributed in churches. In 1720 Pavia had 24,033 inhabitants: there were 11,663 laymen, 10,888 women, 487 priests, and 995 monks.[21] The population of the late 1690s would have been approximately the same. It is possible, if one accepts the high estimate, that enough material on Augustine's bones

19. Ludovico Muratori, *Carteggio a Magliabecchi* (February 11, 1699) (Florence: Olschki, 1975–), 2:373.

20. Maiocchi counted some 130 individual items as related to this controversy. See Maiocchi and Quintavalle, *Anonymi ticinensis,* 41. What exactly Maiocchi included to obtain this number is not made clear. His *Codex Ord. E.S. Augustini Papiae* (5:xx), published in 1915, sidesteps the issue. He makes an uncited reference to Zuradelli, who he says refers to more than 300. Cleonice Baggini's 1913 thesis, "Storia della polemica intorno all'identità della ossa di S. Agostino. . . ," which deals with these works, found 40, that is, a third of Maiocchi's number, an eighth of Zuradelli's. Maiocchi, I infer, was a reader, if not the primary reader, of Baggini's thesis; and given the politicized character of the history department of the university in Pavia, Baggini could not have afforded to criticize a reader's scholarship. If most of what Maiocchi included in his count was published, Pavia was certainly awash in publications concerning Augustine's bones; Zuradelli's number would represent a catastrophic flood.

21. Carlo M. Cipolla, "Profilo di storia demografica della città di Pavia," *Bolletino storico pavese* 6 (1943), 5–87, esp. 54. Thanks to Cipolla we have a very detailed understanding of the population of Pavia. See also his "Per una storia del lavoro in Italia con documenti degli archivi pavesi," *Bolletino storico pavese* 7 (1944), 65–80. See also Giuseppe Aleati, *La populazione di Pavia durante il dominio spagnuolo* (Milan: Giuffrè, 1957), 8, who notes that in 1480 the population was 16,000, and there were some 600 to 700 students; Carla De Rondi, *La populazione della parrocchia di S. Maria in Bethlem di Pavia: il movimento naturale nel settecento* (Milan: Giuffrè, 1983); and Paolo Sala, "Alcune notizie sull'andamento della populazione in Lombardia nel corso del XVIII secolo," in *La populazione italiana nel settecento* (Bologna: Cooperativa Libraria Universitaria Editrice Bologna, 1980), 151–71. In 1730, Milan had 93,600 residents, Pavia 20,494; in 1763 there were 24,286 people in Pavia, according to Sala.

was in print in Pavia for every other person to have a copy of at least one of them. And even if only a fraction of this number actually attended to the controversy, to imagine that 10 or perhaps 20 percent of the population had an interest in this matter and purchased or obtained pamphlets about it is remarkable indeed. Furthermore, given that much of this material was in Latin—granted a simple Latin—such statistics challenge our preconceptions about urban literacy in the early modern period.[22] Given that printers were businessmen seeking to make a profit, there must have been a significant number of individuals who obtained or purchased these works. The numbers of books and pamphlets produced on this topic in Pavia was essentially the same as that found in contemporary controversies taking place in the Netherlands or Paris. In 1700–1701 in Paris, a controversy arose about the last volume of the Benedictine edition of Augustine. It involved thirteen pamphlet publications, a similar number to that printed in Pavia. In Amsterdam, controversies typically involved an equivalent number of items, and the booksellers' shops were said to be full of the pamphlets; a similar phenomenon seems to have taken place in Pavia.[23]

It is easy to imagine that many who claimed to know and could talk a good deal about the controversy in Pavia had not perfected the art of reading but at the same time would profess to be authorities on what was contained in a pamphlet.[24] The reading ability of some might not permit them

22. Roger Chartier has noted that most reading in the French countryside was of traditional, orthodox material. See his "Figures of the 'Other': Peasant Reading in the Age of Enlightenment," in *Cultural History: Between Practices and Representations,* trans. Lydia Cochrane (Cambridge: Polity Press, 1988), 151–71. He refers to an article about rural French readers of the early eighteenth century by Marie-Hélène Froeschlé-Chopard, "Entre peuple et hiérarchie: l'echec d'une pastorale," *Dix-huitième Siècle* 12 (1980), 271–92. As might be expected, Jansenism was a factor in this community of readers. Also informative on these issues are two essays, Dominique Julia, "Reading and the Counter-Reformation," and Roger Chartier, "Reading Matter and 'Popular' Reading: From the Renaissance to the Seventeenth Century," both in *A History of Reading in the West,* ed. Guglielmo Cavallo and Roger Chartier, trans. Lydia G. Cochrane (Amherst: University of Massachusetts Press, 1999), 238–68, esp. 257–69; 269–83.

23. Jonathan Israel, *The Dutch Republic: Its Rise, Greatness, and Fall, 1477–1806* (Oxford: Oxford University Press, 1995), 894–99, describes the Cartesian and Cocceian controversies and the Maresius and Alting controversy in Groningen. The immense controversy of the early 1690s about Balthasar Bekker's *De Betoverde Weereld* (The world bewitched), which involved some 170 publications, was unique at this period; see 929–33.

24. Roger Chartier, "Leisure and Sociability: Reading Aloud in Early Modern Europe," in *Urban Life in the Renaissance* (Newark: University of Delaware Press, 1989), 105–20.

to reproduce a text word for word but would have been adequate for them to explain its gist. Hearing an explanation of what was in a pamphlet from a priest or monk might also help a marginal reader explain the contents to another. The issuance of pamphlets in Italian might act as a control or a corrective to looser interpretations of the ones printed in Latin. Printing was regularly used as a means of official communication between the state and its citizens in Italian cities, and the ability to recognize certain printed nouns would have been an important survival skill for the urban resident. Under the remarkable circumstance of finding the bones, men who claimed not to read were able to identify and draw letters. In an environment where most did not master Latin but heard a good deal of it in religious services, it would be difficult for those without special training to evaluate someone else's language ability.

Scholars are no more prone to admit their own ignorance than anyone else. And in the eighteenth century, they even found it difficult to imagine defects in their favorite authors. Augustine's admission that his Greek was less than perfect was dismissed as modesty. A competence in Hebrew was asserted for him because he knew the local North African dialect of his birthplace; the argument was that this Punic language derived from Phoenician, which was closely related to Hebrew.[25] At universities, cases were reported (granted this was malicious gossip) of teachers of Greek who scarcely knew the language, and of legal instructors who lacked the proper preparation in Latin to teach Roman law. Given the importance of Augustine as a patron saint, and his increased significance for people's daily lives in Pavia, it is to be expected that Pavians would look to the printed words of Colli and Baudini as the way to get the latest news about their patron saint. And, one presumes, there were more people claiming to know what was going on based on the most recent scholarship than had read or even had the training to read the actual publications.

For the Pavian laity, the Invention had reminded them of the need to think beyond the limits of their everyday humanity. Their patron Augustine was not simply an inert piece of their past; the Invention had shown them that the history of their city and its local traditions had an active and vital role in their present and future. And it should not be underestimated

25. Giovanni Lorenzo Berti, *De rebus gestis S. Augustini latinorum patrum nobilissimi librisque ab eodem conscriptis commentarius editus ab humillimo ejus filio* (Venice: Antonio Bassanese, 1756), 6. Joannes Rivius had argued that Augustine was ignorant of Hebrew. Berti refuted this view.

that for the workmen involved in the Invention, for those who experienced miraculous cures, and for their neighbors, one reason for interest in the pamphlets was the simple delight of being able to identify one's own or a friend's name in print.

Colli and Baudini did not write in a vacuum; and, especially in Colli's text, there are indications that the author was reacting to objections and questions and engaging in a dialogue with unspecified auditors. The discovery of the bones had reopened a rift in the historical narrative of the place of Augustine's relics in Pavia's local history. The absence of concrete evidence had allowed rival traditions to be maintained, but the discovery of the bones revealed some of the assumptions underlying the Pavians' conceptions of history. Except for Leva, however, there is an absence of detailed complaints from the supporters of the Canons Regular. Colli and the Augustinian Hermits were accused of being swayed by popular—that is, uninformed—opinion. There seems no reason to doubt the presence of this support, but equally there were no doubt members of the laity who supported the Canons and were skeptical about the so-called Invention proclaimed by the Hermits. The specifics of their activity are much more difficult to identify. Colli was probably responding to questions put directly to him by opponents as well as answering and providing reassurances to the doubts and worries expressed by allies. And we should not forget the argument based on the realities of hard cash. Somebody was paying for all this printed matter. We do not know who printed all of Colli's pamphlets; it may have been Ghidini. Certainly the printer would have expected payment either from sales or in the form of a subvention provided by the author's religious institution or a secular patron. But in either case there would have been an audience for the pamphlets, whether they were purchased or distributed gratis. There appears to be no record of the Hermits funding these texts.

What can be concluded is that by 1699 an audience and a readership of some sort had been created in Pavia for arguments concerning the Augustine Invention. This readership, however, was short-lived, probably ceasing with the published controversy. This runs counter to the view that literacy is a self-evident good that is liberating and an acquisition of lifelong value. The bias of pedagogues inclines one to regard as real readers only those who read throughout their life and to discount those who take up reading for a limited purpose or period of time. A community of readers may have been created in Pavia because unexpectedly a topic appeared that had an appeal to a large segment of the city's population. Augustine, after all, was a patron of the city, and the community's well-being was understood to be dependent on his favor. The posthumous history of Augustine was intertwined with certain aspects of Pavia's sacred and cultural identity. So when a controversy came along involving living members of Pavia's population and one of its major patron saints, and when these issues, which were of genuine interest to Pavia's citizens, were discussed in print, it is not improbable that people brushed up their reading skills or claimed they had had them all along. For them the controversy was a matter of personal interest, very unlike the usual material that could be found for sale in Pavia's bookstores.[26] Most of what was printed in Pavia had its market niches among specialized groups: textbooks for members of the university, manuals on religious practice for members of the clergy, legal texts for lawyers and civil bureaucrats. And, just as likely, when the controversy about Augustine's bones ended, it was to be expected that this popular interest in reading would cease as well. Reading under these circumstances would be like a fad, a trend, or a fashion that would be abandoned for other pursuits.

In 1700 there appeared in Milan a small book or long pamphlet written in Latin of some forty unnumbered pages titled *Dubia quibus rationes pro tumulo & reliquiis nuper compertis die 1. Octobris anno 1695, in confessione Sancti Petri in Coelo Aureo Papiae* (Doubts about the explanations concerning the burial and relics found recently on the first of October 1695 in the crypt of San Pietro in Ciel d'Oro in Pavia).[27] It was published by Giacinto Brenna, heir to the shop of Ludovico Monti, and its author was Giuseppe Maria Bellini, a Canon Regular from Padua. Bellini, who taught in Milan, had made the trip from Milan to Pavia, had done his own investigation, talked to those involved, reviewed what Colli had done, and gone home with a short book in his head. A couple of days later he wrote

26. For example, the theology professor at the university, Giuseppe Girolamo Semenzi, had published an epic poem in Milan in 1686 titled *Il mondo creato.* Early in the eighteenth century, Saccheri would publish his fundamental work on triangles, which proved of importance in the development of non-Euclidean geometries.

27. Giuseppe Maria Bellini, *Dubia quibus rationes pro tumulo & reliquiis nuper compertis die 1. Octobris anno 1695: in confessione Sancti Petri in Coelo Aureo Papiae* (Milan: Giacinto Brenna, 1700). This work also appeared in Bellelli, *Collectio actorum,* 2:208–36.

up his findings.[28] Bellini began his essay by praising the work done so far by Colli and Baudini; but, alas, it simply could not compel acceptance. Certainly, he continued, Pavia's Bishop Lorenzo Trotta had done the right thing by waiting for some decisive evidence before making a decision. But what was the evidence at hand, really? Bellini then started to dismantle what he regarded as Colli's collection of probabilities and distortions. First of all, he observed, there was no so-called moral certainty as to the location of the body. No one knew where the body was, and the documentation in the manuscripts was ambiguous; there was, however, evidence on the other side of the question which Colli chose to ignore. First of all, Colli was too casual in his interpretation of the evidence of the story of Basil and Florentius. The claim that forty years after their "third" Translation the body was returned to its original position came only from modern sources. The oldest and presumably most reliable statements on this matter made no mention of the body's being returned. Furthermore, from Bellini's point of view, the hypothesis that the Translation took place in 1223 lacked any corroborating evidence. He favored placing it back in 773, when the Benedictines were responsible for the body. Thus no blame for hiding the body should be attributed to the Canons.

The second theme to which he devotes a number of chapters concerns where St. Augustine's body was placed. Some sources described the body as being buried very deeply; another referred to a most secret place. None of these would lead an impartial observer to expect the body to appear behind an altar under a couple of paving stones. Given the places where a body could be buried in the crypt of a cathedral, this location was scarcely hidden or secret. Bellini also discussed the confusing language used to describe the location of the body. Some spoke of the "confessorium," others "sub sacello," and some used the Lombard dialect word "scurulum;" all this did was add to the confusion as to where the bones actually were. This vagueness was part of the general problem that nothing about the bones was certain or unambiguous. Then there was the whole issue of dampness in the cathedral: How was it plausible that lettering in charcoal, be it in Italian or Latin, could survive in such a climate? The contradictions of the testimony of the workmen, the lack of consensus as to what letters they saw, were so

28. Muratori, *Carteggio a Magliabecchi* (March 31, 1700), no. 374, 2:424. Muratori mentions the Bellini volume in this letter to Magliabecchi, and one can presume the volume appeared in March, or at least came to Muratori's attention at that time.

obvious that the only practical solution was to toss out such evidence. The glass vials found in the boxes suggested to Bellini that these were the remains of a martyr—hence the ampullae of blood. He even went on to complain about the plain urn that Liutprand was supposed to have used. Wouldn't a king have done better by such an important saint? (Colli would answer this complaint by observing that actually it was really a fine box with which no one could reasonably find fault, given the taste of the time.)

Bellini also took up the issue of Canute's supposed purchase of Augustine's arm. There were several problems, as he saw it. First of all, wasn't it odd that none of the evidence about the sale came from Pavia? Was it likely that such a momentous event as the selling off of one of the most precious relics in the city should pass unnoticed? (To this question Colli would answer that much of the historical record of the past was lost, and that Baronio was a good historian.) But for Bellini the clinching argument came from the list of the bones themselves. For, even granting the truth of the Canute purchase, this could not be St. Augustine. Why? Because the textual record says the king of England bought an arm, not just the forearm, and when a king pays for an arm, he gets the whole thing. One fact the inventory made clear was that only the forearm of the skeleton was missing. So, Bellini argued, whosoever these bones may belong to, some sacred martyr probably, they cannot be assigned to St. Augustine.

Colli fired off a response right after the appearance of Bellini's work: *Identitatis sacrorum ossium d. Augustini ecclesiae doctoris noviter inventorum, ac impugnatorum: defensio* (The identity of the sacred bones of blessed Augustine, Doctor of the Church, recently found (Invented) now impugned: a defense). His essay, a pamphlet of thirty unnumbered pages, broke little new ground. For the most part, he repeated his old arguments as he took up each of Bellini's doubts. He again concluded by restating why all the probabilities he had gathered together added up to the certainty that the relics were indeed those of St. Augustine. Colli presented his argument first by stating each of Bellini's "Doubts" and then giving his refutation of it. Now, it may be that he chose to do this to make clear that he had answered each point and totally dismembered his opponent's argument. It would also suggest that though Bellini's work appeared in nearby Milan, Colli could not presume that his audience would have read it or even seen a copy. This again indicates how localized the intellectual communities and their controversies were during this period. Here Colli first clearly stepped beyond his earlier role, which had been, in part, to articulate the excitement of those Pavians involved in the discovery of the bones and in determining their significance. With Bellini's *Dubia* and Colli's response, we have the beginning of an intellectual controversy. This debate had a life of its own which was disconnected from the perceptions and participation of the Pavian laity and clergy who were readers but not authors. This change of discourse represents one of those little crises of old regime Europe: Who answered to whom? Who had more power on the local scene, centralized authorities or local elites? How open should controversies be, and who should resolve them? And what role should the people, however that term was understood, play in this competition for authority and the right to issue judgments?

At this point a major Italian scholar entered into the controversy, a Benedictine named Giovanni Gaspare Beretti.[29] Beretti was the philosophy professor at the University of Pavia. If the Canons wouldn't listen to the historian Ghisoni, perhaps they would yield to the voice of philosophy. Beretti had finished his 237-page book on August 15, the Feast of the Assumption in 1700; it was titled *Lynchnus chronologico-juridicus ad discutiendas tenebras, seu Dubia quibus rationes pro tumulo, & reliquiis nuper compertis 1. Octob. anno 1695. in Confessione S. Petri in Caelo aureo Papiae ventilantur expressa A.P.D. Joseph Maria Bellini Patavino in Congregatione Lateranensi Canonico, S. Theologiae lectore, eisdem iterum ediitis, ac ex integro hic ad autographi fidem insertis pro sac. ossium M.D. Aurelii Augustini ep. et doct. ac regii Ticini protectoris identitate vindicanda, at illustranda* (The lamp of judicial chronology dispersing the shadows or the Doubts concerning the arguments about the burial and relics recently discovered on October 1, 1695, in the crypt of San Pietro in Ciel d'Oro in Pavia which were openly aired by Giuseppe Maria Bellini, theology teacher of Padua and of the Congregation of the Canons Regular of the Lateran . . .). His book did not list a publisher or place of publication, but it was dedicated to a member of the Milanese nobility, Cesare de Pagani, and it was probably pub-

29. Armando Petrucci, "Beretti, Giovanni Gaspare," in *Dizionario biografico degli italiani*, 9:59–61. Petrucci argues that "Beretti" is the proper spelling of his name, not "Beretta," as in the eighteenth century. I have followed him in this. See also G. Castagna, "La corrispondenza dei monaci benedettini cassinesi col Muratori," *Benedictina* 6 (1952), 270–86; 7 (1953), 61–84; 9 (1955), 249–80; 10 (1956), 121–41; 11 (1957), 97–108. A. Capelli, *Il P. Beretta e una lettera ined. del Muratori* (Modena, 1890).

lished in Milan and funded by the Hermits of San Pietro. Beretti's aim was to elevate the controversy from the discourse of local antiquarians to that of the genuine historical research done by elite scholars such as himself. Beretti indeed entered the controversy in the guise of what we would recognize as an intellectual. As he saw his role, it was to demonstrate what was significant and genuinely at stake in the Pavian quarrel. A modern reader is apt to find what he claimed was thoughtful broad-mindedness to be actually narrow and cut off from other more significant social realities to which Colli and perhaps Leva gave imperfect articulation. Beretti did not worry whether his views would reach beyond a small number of polemicists; he simply presumed that popular acceptance would promptly follow his clear statement of the correct resolution of the issues. As a Benedictine, he believed himself to be above and outside local interests. Above all, Beretti believed that it was the responsibility of scholars and experts like himself to set straight whose bones these were.

Beretti had had an early interest in what was going on in San Pietro since Colli had asked him to prepare a *votum* in 1699. Beretti made it clear from the beginning that his intellectual discourse was cosmopolitan. He quoted from Pascal's *Pensées* and indicated that he understood the purpose of the famous doubt of Descartes. He saw himself as elevating a controversy that had been conducted on a plebeian level to one of patrician dignity.[30] His aim was to review all the evidence afresh to see if Bellini's arguments had merit. But from the beginning he could not forgo the opportunity to diminish the reputation of the Canons Regular and to elevate his own order, the Benedictines. The rivalry between these orders was an ancient one, and each claimed priority over the other. Beretti observed that all the doubts and ambiguities surrounding Augustine's relics had been caused by the actions of the Canons Regular; the Benedictines were not to blame.

Who were Basil and Florentius? he asked. Were they even two people? The Chronicle of Brescia seemed to make them one person, and there was no evidence they were Benedictines, so a date before the thirteenth century for their Translation was impossible. And anyway, whoever they were or whatever order they belonged to, besides moving St. Augustine's body, we are also told that they hid Boethius' body. But we know Boethius' body was exhumed in the early sixteenth century: according to Gualla, the body

30. E. P. Thompson, "Patrician Society, Plebeian Culture," *Journal of Social History* 7 (1974), 382–405.

was clearly identifiable because the remains were dressed in the fashion of a Roman senator and the head was missing. (Gualla, the source of this information, had presumed that Boethius was beheaded by Theodosius, though his torture was more inhumane than that, involving the crushing of his skull with tightened cords.) If Boethius' body had been returned, surely the same thing was done with Augustine. If not, what sense can be made of the concern shown about concealing Augustine in 1525, the time of one French invasion, and in 1527 with the second French attack? If the body was lost in the church or concealed elsewhere, of what use had been all this talk about moving Augustine's relics to a safe place? One parenthetical observation suggests itself as a consequence of Beretti's analysis: What had happened in 1695 wasn't an Invention at all. Augustine had been moved about, but his relics had never been lost. The excitement of October 1 had been misplaced and needed redirecting. Or, to phrase it differently, the mythic symbolic language of Invention that had made sense of the spontaneous experience of finding St. Mark was no longer an appropriate discourse, at least for the relics of Augustine.

Beretti made a detailed analysis of all the manuscript sources. He worried over the document Ghisoni had attributed to Sigisbert, of whom nothing was known. Bellini had made a good deal of this Sigisbert, and Beretti ridiculed this attribution as well, using these problems to show that he was familiar with Mabillon's method. Beretti was also willing to accept nontextual evidence: he gave credence to the story that in 1579 a possessed or crazy man indicated that there was a powerful spiritual presence in the crypt altar. He reported the miraculous sixteenth-century cure of a man brought to the *arca* after having received a severe bite from a serpent. He also gathered what information was known about eighth-century burials, the coffins that were used, and the objects placed in them. He believed that the workmen had indeed seen writing on the marble box, and from their description he was willing to identify it as in what he called a Gothic script. Whenever he was unable to refute completely one of Bellini's objections, he observed that the evidence was sometimes ambiguous. He reviewed anatomical theories and considered different reckonings of how many bones a human body possesses, and he accepted the view that there are 477.

He could not conclude his work without returning to an issue of personal importance—the defamation of the Canons Regular. In his penultimate chapter he attacked the standard view on the origins of the Canons as elaborated by their seventeenth-century historian, Pennotto. As I mentioned earlier, Pennotto dated the beginning of their order to 391, when Valerius, the bishop of Hippo, gave to Augustine the garden adjacent to his church to be the site of his future monastery. Pennotto argued that this was Augustine's first religious order, the Canons Regular. Beretti intervened to demonstrate that what Pennotto claimed about the Canons and the Augustinian Rule (Regula) was false because the Rule was simply a general guide for right living and made no reference to a specific religious order. The Canons could not claim priority over the Hermits. The foundation of the Canons must have come much later and did not derive directly from Augustine. Certainly they were preceded by the Benedictines.

These tenaciously defended traditions about the foundation of orders played a significant part in defining their traits and characteristics. We may have a bias toward regarding such quarrels as trivial and removed from appropriate religious discourse; we have an easier time seeing them as political struggles over turf rather than as the consequence of strong and complex religious feelings. Surprisingly, such beliefs are frequently the kind of thing a group or organization can give up with no damage to continuance of the institution. And, as we saw in the twentieth century, both the Canons Regular and the Augustinian Hermits had no difficulty abandoning this myth of origin. But the willingness to quarrel about traditions is one of the things that keep traditions alive. Beretti's view was that the controversy was occasioned by error; proper knowledge of historical fact and the discovery of the true moment of origin would remove the irrational. His ecclesiastical history was not about conflict and controversy between mighty opposites, or the tragic story told by an idiot, but concerned instead fretful, forgetful, and overly ambitious groups trying to usurp the rightful place of others. This kind of analysis showed Beretti to be completely out of touch with the peculiarities and quirks of local church histories. He believed in the actual, factual importance of origins—and, sad to say, the Canons did not have as illustrious a beginning as the Benedictines. Nor had Augustine gone through the rather sloppy procedure of being lost and invented. But the bones were his: that much Beretti would grant to tradition.

Shortly after Beretti's work appeared, a Franciscan spoke up for Colli and the relics; this was Alberto Castellano, a teacher of theology. His Latin pamphlet, consisting of twenty-six unnumbered pages, was titled *Identitatis sacrorum ossium nuper in crypteo sacello apud S. Petro in Caelo Aureo Ticini Regii Scurolo dicto repertorum satis probata, ad illius oppositorem: paraenesis* (The identity of the sacred bones recently found in the crypt altar in San Pietro in Ciel d'Oro in Pavia reported to be in the so-called Royal Crypt, against those who oppose it: an update). The pamphlet was published in Milan. A rumor was spread that Colli was in fact the author of this work as well; there seems to be no reason to accept this, but it does indicate that gossip continued about the controversy over the relics. Castellano had been one of the individuals who submitted a *votum* in 1699. His statement at that time included some citations from Augustine's works, although this was not the case with most of the *vota,* which simply endorsed the relics without reference to any sources or scholarly citations. Castellano, unusual for participants in this controversy, had a wide knowledge of Augustine's writings. He began his pamphlet by explaining Augustine's views on quarrels, how they should be conducted, and how doubts should be investigated. He had a particular ax to grind, and that was his wish to defend some of the authors Bellini had attacked. He was also defensive about the reputation of Vincent of Beauvais, whose reliability had been questioned. He reviewed the variety of documentation and the manuscripts used by Bellini. Unsurprisingly he was critical and found fault with the texts supportive of the Canons and those who doubted the identity of the relics. Where the evidence supporting Colli and the Hermits was problematic, he argued that it was unreasonable to expect precise documentation from such a remote time.

Bellini was not willing to allow these reactions to go unanswered. In 1702 he published a refutation aimed primarily at Beretti, but it also mentioned Colli and Castellano. The lengthy title began *Responsio apologetica ad Lynchnum Chronologico-juridicum* (Justification and response to the Judicial-Chronological Lamp) and continued with the rest of Beretti's title. The work, a book of 214 pages, claimed to be published by the Anisson firm in Lyon. This, however, was a false place of publication; the book was probably printed, like his previous work, in Milan, or perhaps Venice.[31]

31. According to the *Giornale de'Letterati* 3 (1710), 352, it was published in Venice. Although this was ten years after the event, the editors of the *Giornale* knew their publishing community. The conventions on the use of false places of publication in Italy differed from the practice in England. See Michael Treadwell, "On False and Misleading Imprints in the London Book Trade, 1660–1750," in *Fakes and Frauds: Varieties of Deception in Print and*

Anisson's establishment was well known to Italians informed about the international book trade. His shop produced books of interest to Italian scholars, and the firm's correspondence with scholars like Magliabecchi in Florence facilitated an easy exchange of scholarly news between France and Italy. Bellini may have used the false location because he was under some sort of pressure from civil or ecclesiastical authorities, but he did not adopt other subterfuges such as using a pseudonym or publishing anonymously. His motive may just as likely have been in the opposite direction: he or the publisher may have hoped to benefit from the cachet of foreign publication. Perhaps the decision not to use Venice as the place of publication, if that was what happened, was influenced by the international scene. Venice was seeking to remain neutral in the life-and-death struggle over the disputed inheritance of the Spanish Empire. The French and Spanish were preparing to face the German Empire, the Dutch, and the English. French administrators serving Spain's new Bourbon king, Philip V, had arrived in Lombardy. This may not have seemed the right time for Venice to appear eager to intervene in a Lombard quarrel.

Listing a false place of publication probably would not have impeded acquisition of the book in Milan or Pavia; only those outside the local area might be misled and then be frustrated in their attempts to obtain the book from Lyon. Bellini may also have chosen this strategy because he was answering a work that had no acknowledged place of publication. He made clear from the beginning of this book that he was allied with the innovative intellectual community developing in Venice, and he mentioned Apostolo Zeno as his most significant supporter. Zeno had established himself as one of Italy's foremost Humanist scholars and as the leader of the movement to reform poetry and opera libretti by returning to more classical models. As a sign of Bellini's open-mindedness, he cited the Anglican Archbishop Usher's chronology of world history, the French Bodin's *Methodus,* and the Venetian Sarpi's *De beneficiis,* a work on the Index.

Part of Zeno's cultural project was to restore Italian scholarship, under the leadership of Venice, to its former pristine condition and reputation. It was not surprising that Bellini, in this spirit, would want to show both that he understood the advances made by the French Benedictines and that he had the intellectual independence to recognize and correct their

Manuscript, ed. Robin Myers and Michael Harris (Winchester: St. Paul's Bibliographies, 1989), 29–46.

errors. Therefore he cited the ecclesiastical historians Charles Le Cointe and Noël d'Alexandre, and used them to correct Mabillon.[32] This kind of exercise served to establish his credentials and support his claim to be an authority. Bellini could not bring himself to overlook Beretti's assault on the origins of the Canons Regular, and so he began his book by reasserting the truth of the Canons' origins in Valerius' garden in 391. Did this mean, he speculated, that Benedict's Rule and the Benedictine order itself derive from the Canons Regular as created by Augustine?

Bellini went over the same ground everyone had been sifting through. The problem, as he saw it, with those who argued for the authenticity of the relics was that they selected those bits of a document that supported their so-called Invention but forgot all the rest. What was one to make of a document that described the location fairly well, but then elaborated that the burial place was richly decorated and full of jewels? If the text were to believed about the location, how could it be so wrong about the description of what was buried with the body? Was it describing the same thing? And, in fact, all the alleged evidence about the location of the body was confused, vague, and contradictory. Each bit of evidence on its own seemed to speak persuasively and knowledgeably, but all the little differences and contradictions with the rest of the facts undermined confidence. Bellini's position, in certain respects, echoed that of Beretti. Obviously, he would agree that this was no Invention, and, one gathers, he believed that none was possible. In this work there was no suggestion that Bellini believed the Canons could actually produce the real body if they wanted to. Beretti found no cause for amazement in the so-called Invention because authentic records proved the continuous presence of the relics in the crypt altar. He concluded that the only thing the authentic records made clear was that no one knew exactly where the relics of Augustine were. No supposed Invention or outbreak of miracles could discredit that fact. Bellini thus demonstrated the same aristocratic disdain for his opponents as had Beretti.

Bellini's assessment of the evidence is much more detailed in this book, but his analysis opens up little that was actually new. He did, however, for good measure insult Beretti, claiming to find his Latin laughable and his style to be that of an Esau. He spent more time ruminating on the preposterousness of relying on the testimony of stonemasons about the writ-

32. On this general topic, see Waquet, *Le modèle français et l'Italie savante.*

ing allegedly found on the marble box. In any event, he said, such an investigation could more profitably rely on the experimental method of Bacon making use of the chemical laboratory of Robert Boyle. Was it even possible for charcoal writing to last in such a place? An experiment was needed, and the chemist's lab might provide the answer. Bellini's conclusion was that the only prudent course with all these doubtful matters was skepticism. The relics as described were probably those of a martyr, Bellini asserted; the presence of the rose-colored glass vials was typical of such burials. Montfauçon's *Diarium* was published in Paris in 1702, and knowledge of it must have become available fairly soon after, if only through book review journals. Montfauçon implicitly supported Bellini.

In the following year, 1703, Mario Callini, a Canon Regular, published in Italian a pamphlet of forty unnumbered pages which in large measure restated the position of Bellini. But Callini was in fact a pseudonym for Bernardino Trevisan, a Venetian Jesuit.[33] In 1699 he had published an Augustinian work on the soul, *L'immortalità dell'anima,* which was part of a longer work that he completed in 1704, his *Meditazioni filosofiche.* It was later reviewed by the Venetian journal *Galleria di Minerva* in 1707. Trevisan was a new light on the Venetian intellectual scene with a reputation as a creative thinker and the owner of an impressive library. His work under the name Callini was published in Cremona by Lorenzo Ferrari and titled *Motivi che sforzano a dubitare se le reliquie scoperte nella confessione di S. Pietro siano identiche con l'ossa sacratissime del Padre Sant'Agostino* (The motives that compel doubt as to whether the relics discovered in the crypt of San Pietro are identical with the most sacred bones of our Father St. Augustine).[34] Cremona was famous for its church dedicated to St. Augustine; Pavia and Cremona both claimed him as their patron. Presuming that this work was indeed published in Cremona, it is remarkable that the title page no longer needed to specify that the location of the quarrel was San Pietro's in Pavia: the controversy had acquired a wide notoriety. The connection of these last two books to Venice indicated a concerted effort by the Venetians to hijack at least part of the controversy.

Callini praised the good sense of the Canons, whose sole aim, he said, was to bring the people back to their senses and to make them worthy of

33. This information is given in the *Giornale de'Letterati* 3 (1710), 354. Its judgment is to be relied on.

34. Bellelli, *Collectio actorum,* 2:237–302.

true religiosity. The Canons were slow to accept the identity of the relics not because they were skeptics but because they were not apt to be tricked by passing enthusiasms. Speculation was inappropriate on such an important matter; the sincere religious individual must proceed with a wary caution. Trevisan regarded Beretti as the only serious scholar to have defended the identity of the relics, but even the Benedictine could not make a persuasive case for them. Although it was not an occasion for much disagreement, Trevisan returned to the evidence of the first two Translations. His primary interest was to show his competence as a reader of documents. A letter from a Lucedo Prete cited by some sources in connection with the Sardinian translation was clearly bogus because it used an anno Domini date, but such dates were not in use at that time. He also described the paintings in the Chapel of St. Aphian that contained images of the Basil and Florentius Translation. In addition to this visual record, he reviewed all of the manuscript evidence and concluded that it was hopelessly confused and contradictory. He concurred with Bellini that from 1527 to 1697 the testimonies produced about the location of the body simply did not agree. Trevisan could not refrain from observing that there were often problems with this sort of thing. The famous discovery of the intact body—or was it just a skeleton—of St. Bartholomew in Benevento made it difficult to understand how his skin, his tanned hide, located in Rome, had been separated from the rest of him and yet both were in such a perfect and complete state of preservation.

What new science, he wondered, would have to come from London and the laboratory of Boyle to explain how scribbles made from charcoal could endure for centuries on damp marble? How was one to assess the testimony of bricklayers and diggers? Was their ignorance to teach the learned the burial places of the saints? Trevisan claimed to fear that a decision about this whole matter might be put in the hands of some Protestant English surgeon who would inspect the relics at Coventry or Canterbury and decide how much of an arm Canute had purchased. He was apparently unaware that the relic had been destroyed in the attempt to purify English churches, perhaps in the late 1530s, or more likely during Cromwell's regime. His implicit argument was that the controversialists needed to proceed with greater caution lest some external authority be brought in to settle the issue. Trevisan did not expect his sophisticated readers to be seriously worried that English scientists would be appealed to for a solution. The real danger lay closer to home: an appeal to Rome might result in the imposition of an answer by fiat about what was a matter of fact instead of being answered as it should be by the debate of trained scholars. It was equally counterproductive to call in either English chemists or Roman pontiffs. The mere presence of miracles, Trevisan noted, proved nothing; they might not be validated, and even so, sometimes their source remained unknown. Trevisan invoked the standards set by the Council of Trent to evaluate relics. By such a standard it might be claimed that a sacred burial had been recovered, but there was no reason to identify it as that of St. Augustine.

Shortly after the appearance of this book, an Augustinian Hermit of Pavia named Mario Serafino Tragopa prepared a manuscript attacking Callini/Trevisan.[35] Although he was incensed about what Callini/Trevisan had said about Augustine's relics, his greatest wrath was directed against the Canons Regular. Tragopa doesn't argue, he shouts. One of his grounds for dismissing the arguments of Callini/Trevisan and Bellini was that they cited Noël Alexandre, some of whose works had been condemned by the Index, and they mentioned the Bollandists' *Acta sanctorum,* which was condemned by the Spanish Inquisition. Tragopa refers to a *votum* he wrote on the relics of St. Augustine, though it did not appear in the *Vota* edition of 1699. This would suggest that in addition to the statements published by Colli, others circulated as well. And though we cannot know for certain, this manuscript may also have been passed around: supporters of the Augustinian Hermits would certainly have enjoyed it.

In 1704, now in his early eighties, Michele Colli once again appeared in print arguing for the authenticity of the relics found in San Pietro, this time in a pamphlet of thirty-eight pages written in Italian, published by Carlo Francesco Magri of Pavia, under the title *Sommario o sii compendio di tutte le ragione addotte sin'ora; purgate & illustrate dalle nubi di dubii, eccitati ultimamente nella grande scrittura volgare dell'aversarii* (Summary or compendium of all the reasons adopted up to now; purged and elucidated from the clouds of doubts, excited most recently by opponents writing in Italian). The Latin edition, with the title *Commentariolum,* was also printed by Magri; this is a book of some two hundred pages.[36] Here Colli makes

35. BNPav Mss. Ticinensis 32. 9, "Rifletti di Mario Serafino Tragopa sopra un scritto di P. Mario Callini," 15 unnumbered leaves.

36. This work by Colli is included in a list of new books which appeared in the Venetian journal *Galleria di Minerva* 7 (1707), art. 9, 221. This notice is the closest Colli came to having his work reviewed.

public the strange case of the Canon Ferdinand Leva, who had abandoned his attacks against Colli because of a dream-vision of St. Augustine. But most of what Colli has to offer had appeared before. Shortly afterward Colli died. This publication marks the Pavian ending of this second phase of the controversy.

It is worth noting that another four thousand to perhaps twelve thousand items were published in Pavia, Milan, Cremona, and perhaps Venice during this phase of the controversy. Some of these were books of several hundred pages. What effect did the availability of so much information and disputation have on the community in Pavia? Its relation with a patron saint and his patronage networks are not directly accessible. One of Colli's arguments for recognition was that Pavians had already begun to worship the relics, and, as he said, what was to be gained by delay? The relics were genuine, and it was only jealousy that allowed this ambiguous situation to continue. The failure to reach a decision gave the false impression of encouraging the local laity to do what it wanted to do. Colli's solution was to authorize the worship of the relics. Presumably, however, there were others who listened to the Canons and were appalled at the impious and overly bold behavior of the Hermits and their lay supporters.

In this second phase of the controversy, it is more difficult to point to traces of conversations of authors with Pavian readers. The interchange, for the most part, had become one between authors. The greater range of the places of publication, the adoption of pseudonyms, and the elaboration of the controversy to include disputes beyond the context of San Pietro suggest changes in potential readership. It is easy to imagine Pavians wanting to own and to consume pamphlets and short books about an issue they cared about, written by authors they knew. The motivation to look seriously at and even purchase the books of Beretti or Bellini would require a different, more sophisticated level of involvement.[37] One may presume that, if only because of their expense, the books would have had a more restricted readership than the pamphlets. To be sure, the acquisition of a folio or multivolume set would be outside the reach of most incomes, but no books in the controversy had yet appeared in this format. The purchase price of a book like that of Beretti or Bellini may be com-

37. On the issue of owners not reading their books, I note that the leaves of Beretti's *Lynchnus* were uncut when I looked at the copy in the Biblioteca Nazionale in Florence. Its owner was interested enough to keep it but not to read it.

pared with what a modern family might spend to attend a professional sporting event or visit a theme park.

The impression one gains in reading through the second phase of the controversy is that the issue or debate was being taken out of the control of the Pavians. Indeed, it seems as if the new, vibrant intellectual leaders of the Venetian cultural world succeeded in taking it over. Although the exact date is not known, Colli seems to have died shortly after the publication of his 1704 *Sommario.* He would have been in his mid-eighties at this time. In any event, no one carried on the controversy or took up Colli's mantle. In 1706 the French and Spanish administrators of Lombardy were driven out and replaced by a new regime under the direction of the Austrian Hapsburgs. In this period of political uncertainty local interest in the controversy disappeared, and it fell into the hands of the book review editors. The books about the authenticity of the bones were reviewed in the third volume of the *Giornale de'Letterati* for 1710. The *Giornale* had begun publication that same year in Venice; its editors were Scipione Maffei, Antonio Vallisnieri, and Apostolo Zeno. The journal, which appeared quarterly, was devoted to promoting and advertising works of Italian learning to a European audience. Special emphasis was given to erudite books, especially those on the Italian Middle Ages inspired by Mabillon's methods, to experimental works of natural philosophy, and to volumes devoted to reforming Italian letters and poetry. The article on the controversy was a straightforward summary, though it is clear that the author was skeptical that these were the relics of St. Augustine.

A more nuanced understanding of the message of the article in the *Giornale* requires a comparison of this article with the two adjacent to it. The *Giornale* had to deal with ecclesiastical subjects with some care. Offended parties might well seek aid from powerful patrons in Rome; hence the *Giornale*'s somewhat circumspect approach. The editors were not opposed to controversy, so long as good scholarship, in their view, and not appeals to authority, won out in the end. The sixth, seventh, and eighth articles of the third issue all review controversies, and each discusses a number of different works and authors. The first article concerns Giusto Fontanini's defense of Mabillon's historical method. This dispute had been sparked by the Jesuit P. Germon's *De veteribus regum francorum diplomatibus et arte secernendi antiqua diplomata vera a falsis Ad R. P.*

Mabillonium disceptatio (The Documents and Charters of the Old Kings of France and the Method of Determining the True Ones from the False: A Disputation with the Reverend Father Mabillon) of 1703. Fontanini had been supported by Domenico Passionei and Benedetto Bacchini. In part the *Giornale*'s purpose was to attack the French journal of the Jesuits, the *Journal de Trévoux*; as the Italians saw it, even the Protestant *Acta eruditorum* was more fair-minded in its consideration of Mabillon than the Jesuit journal. The editors of the *Giornale* were delighted to discuss the Italian scholars who defended Mabillon and Fontanini. Although the quarrel was in some measure a controversy between religious orders, the debate was conducted within the bounds of historical evidence, and the winner was easy to call. The third controversy, in the eighth article, was a collection of the responses generated by Muratori's proposal to change the standards of taste in evaluating Italian poetry, *Della perfetta poesia italiana.* Here too the controversialists carried on a civil exchange in accordance with the principles of the Republic of Letters as they were understood in Venice. Muratori had appealed to traditional secular, aristocratic values associated with the Arcadian movement. This too was something the Venetian editors approved of and in which they could expect Venice to take the dominant role.

The Pavian controversy, in contrast, was not up to par, and most of the controversialists did not understand the basic principles of historical argument. The situation was not yet under the control of the Venetians. The review began not with the Invention but with a description of how San Pietro came to be divided between the Canons and the Augustinian Hermits, emphasizing that there were two different histories, and each religious order had its own account or social memory. Both the Canons and the Hermits had selected the events that explained their perception of the history of San Pietro. The writings of the controversy expressed the collective memories of the rival orders. According to the editors of the *Giornale,* the controversialists were trapped in the traditions of these rival interpretations. The individual authors influenced and were influenced by the social memory of the order each supported.[38] The Pavian controversy

38. This method and vocabulary, used to analyze much larger social groups, was developed by the sociologist Maurice Halbwachs in his 1925 work *Les cadres sociaux de la mémoire,* titled in English *The Collective Memory* (New York: Harper and Row, 1980). The concept was further refined by Marc Bloch. The discussions of such mentalities is central to the analysis of social structure, ideology, and religious symbols.

never really rose above the level of fraternal disputes in the opinion of the *Giornale.* The implicit conclusion of the review was that an impartial resolution of the controversy was possible, to be determined by impartial historians. Or, as we might express it, they believed that the controversy could be resolved, but only by those who had the social memory of Venetian intellectual like themselves.

While they could not say so directly, the Venetian editors could see that this controversy was heading in only one direction: an appeal to Rome. But an appeal to authority was not the way to resolve what was a matter of fact or evidence. It was this kind of appeal that had earned the Catholic faith such notoriety in the Galileo affair, and the *Giornale* editors were eager to avoid a repetition. The best way to prevent this was for elite scholars to manage such disputes themselves. Controversial matters should be debated by competent practitioners of the appropriate scientific discipline. There was a place for papal authority and regulation, but the determination of matters of historical fact was not one of them.[39] The review closed by noting what Montfauçon had said in his *Diarium:* he did not want to make a judgment about the relics because the evidence was not there. This negative freedom, "in piena libertà" to leave a question open was at the heart of the reviewers conception of the scholarly freedom of aristocrats like themselves. The aim of the *Giornale* had been to silence the other controversialists and to shame them into accepting the restraint exemplified by the Venetian position.

Book review journals like the *Giornale* were comparatively new on the intellectual scene, and their audience was clearly not the sort of new readers who may have appeared in Pavia. Of course, any reader might dip into a review and extract something from it, but so much of the prevailing cultural horizon was presumed as common knowledge by the editors and reviewers that they tended to exclude casual readers. The first such journal, the French *Journal des Sçavans,* had begun publishing in January 1665. An Italian journal appeared in Rome in 1666 but had ceased regular

39. To be sure, the Venetians were not so foolish as to make an explicit statement about the precise limits of the purview of the papacy in such matters. The history of religious houses was full of controversies over rights, privileges, customs, and traditions. Robert Kendrick, in chap. 4 of his *Celestial Sirens* (Oxford: Clarendon Press, 1996), 90–105, describes the controversy that broke out between two rival choirs of nuns at Santa Marta in Milan. The controversy was of such bitterness that it was referred to Rome several times for adjudication. The Venetian editors had no quarrel with the papacy's deciding such matters.

publication by the end of the 1670s. Benedetto Bacchini launched a second *Giornale* from Parma, which appeared from 1686 to 1689 and irregularly in the 1690s. The 1710 Venice *Giornale* was its successor. The primary purpose of the French *Journal* was to sort out the variety of publications being produced in Paris; it paid scant attention to books published elsewhere. This was also the practice of journals in the Netherlands; their primary purpose was to advertise significant productions of local publishers. The only journals that reviewed a majority of books that were published outside their local market were the *Acta eruditorum* of Leipzig and Bacchini's *Giornale*. The 1710 *Giornale* defined its role as presenting the work of Italian scholars to the European scholarly world as well as to other Italians. Such a journal was addressed to those who were regular readers and were interested in the bibliographic context of scholarship. The occasional reader and others in Pavia who were specifically interested in the controversy over Augustine's bones were not likely to read the 1710 *Giornale*. No one published a refutation of the *Giornale* article.[40] The *Giornale* had connections with Pavia and had its own distributor, but there is no indication of any reaction to the review.[41]

There were no civil troubles caused in Pavia by the failure to recognize the relics found in San Pietro to be those of St. Augustine. Complaints were made that some members of the laity were treating the relics as authentic and were worshipping them and showing them reverence. But no effective steps seem to have been taken to discipline or correct this behavior. No reaction to the Invention of the kind that, in the past, had played such a significant role in the spontaneous renewal of faith and of certain cultural symbols arose to repair the broken community in the church of San Pietro. As we have seen, the situation there was more complicated than a conflict between the desire of the laity for control over their local church versus the desire of a central authority in Rome to assert its power. Perhaps the dichotomous nature of the cathedral's inhabitants precluded any local solution other than exhausted silence.

In the published controversy, both sides accepted the principle that oral

40. In *Vico's cultural history*, 160–66, I describe the famous controversy that took place in Naples between the *Giornale* and Vico concerning the review of his *De antiquissima*. See Giambattista Vico, *On the Most Ancient Wisdom of the Italians*, trans. L. M. Palmer (Ithaca: Cornell University Press, 1988), which includes the text, the review, and the ensuing debate.

41. Brendan Dooley, *Science, Politics, and Society in Eighteenth-Century Italy: The "Giornale de'Letterati" and Its World* (New York: Garland, 1991).

tradition and custom needed to be supplemented by documents that could be used to construct a consistent account of and a coherent approach to the evidence. Each side could refer to a story or point of view that would be complete and continuous if not for the ravages of time, which had destroyed important records of the past. The Augustinian Hermits and the Canons Regular had developed rival histories of their place in the cultural tradition of St. Augustine and of Pavia. Both incorporated what we might call mythic elements in the way they presented their cultural tradition and the documentation they believed supported their Rule and their way of life. For the communities involved in the controversy, the surprise appearance of relics that might be St. Augustine's disoriented rather than clarified how each understood the relationship of their attitudes to oral and written traditions. In 1710 the Venetian journalists summarized what was known about the controversy, and they used it to further Venice's interests in continuing its long-standing conflict with papal authority. Despite the apparent truce, the issue of the authenticity of the bones remained unresolved.

FOUR
The Controversy Renewed and Resolved

IN 1724 a Dominican, Pietro Francesco Orsini, was elected pope, and because he was a Dominican, some hoped he would show some favor toward the Jansenists.[1] He took the name Benedict XIV, but changed it to XIII because the previous Benedict XIII had been an anti-pope and should not have counted. Six months after his election, on November 6, 1724, he confirmed the teaching of the Council of Trent on grace, human freedom, God's foreknowledge, the legitimacy of the teaching of both Augustine and Aquinas, and the traditional advice to interpret Augustine in the light of Aquinas. This statement of principle was contained in an official letter he wrote to the Dominican order. It made clear that there was to be no yielding on the issue of Jansenism. This position implicitly rejected Bayle's clever *jeu* and officially severed Augustine's thought from the unanswerable questions that gave such energy to Jansenist-inspired reflections about man, God, salvation, and damnation.

On January 23, 1728, Benedict took up in an official manner the issue relevant to Pavia—the question of Augustine's bones. He sent Pavia's bishop Francesco Pertusati a letter on the matter, instructing him to reopen the investigation of the saint's relics. The pope wanted a definitive answer in six months, and the inference was that he expected a positive identification, for why else pursue the matter? Benedict did not intend to resolve all disputes between the Canons and the Hermits, nor to end Pope John XXII's curious attempt to institutionalize strife and dissonance in a religious building. He accepted the division of San Pietro with its two chapter houses, opposite entrances, and separate stairways into the crypt, all established seemingly to facilitate the quarrel between the orders and their rival traditions. The pope wanted unity only on the issue of Augustine's relics, and he wanted their authenticity confirmed; he forbade any controversy while the matter was being adjudicated. He would have no truck with the posi-

1. Gaspare de Caro, "Benedetto XIII," in *Dizionario biografico degli italiani*, 8:384–93.

tion promoted by the Venetian journalists that the interests of true religion were best served by a free investigation, that is, one conducted under their auspices. He had no objection to free investigations into historical matters, but questions of worship and liturgical practices were the responsibility of the judicial procedures determined and administered in Rome. The Venetians, by claiming that they, or at least their historians, had a legitimate voice in such disputes, were simply continuing, in a less overtly contentious manner, the quarrels of a century earlier between Venice and Rome.

The worship of saints, relics, and sacred images had become a crucial concern of the papacy, whose preeminence in these matters had been confirmed at the Council of Trent. A local diocese acting in conjunction with, or rather under the direction of, Rome might prepare a case for a change or innovation in saintly worship. From his years of experience working with the daily religious concerns of his diocese, Benedict knew the importance of saints in local religious practice and understood how the proper cultivation of this worship could ensure that the authority and paternal influence of Rome would be felt at the parish level. Benedict as pope was unusual in his commitment to the spiritual life of the local priests of the diocese of Rome. In 1725 he held a council of the provincial clergy of Rome in St. John Lateran.[2] This synod, and his use of local synods in general as means to reform and improve local religious practice, offered a significant example of his hope of implementing the decisions of Trent. Benedict had no local knowledge of Pavia, but his actions appear to have been supported by the local laity. In keeping with his belief in Rome's primacy on the matter of liturgy and sainthood, we learn scarcely anything of Pavian sentiments from the official documents resolving the issue of the authenticity of the bones. This did not mean that he was indifferent to local concerns; he knew how to accommodate Roman universalism to parochial interests.

The situation in Pavia had been brought to Benedict's attention in 1727 during a visitation to Benevento. He was informed of the discovery of Augustine's relics and the fact that they had not been officially authenticated. He then ordered the head of the Augustinian Hermits, Fulgenzio Bellelli,

2. The unusual character of this event was noted by contemporaries. The biography prepared on Benedict's death devotes some 80 of its 1,900 pages to this council. See *Das Ruhm-und Wunderwürdige leben und Thaten Pabts Benedicti des Dreizehenden* (Frankfurt: Ben. Christoph Riegel, 1731), 442–516.

to go to Pavia and expedite the matter. Bellelli was a Neapolitan born in 1675 or 1677—the date is disputed.[3] He had entered the Augustinian Hermits in Naples and had lived in Rome, Siena, and Florence. He first made his reputation in 1711 with the *Mens S. Augustini,* printed in Antwerp; it was a fairly straightforward Augustinian work that, among other things, demonstrated Augustine's orthodoxy—that is, that Augustine was not a Jansenist. After having served as secretary for the order since 1720, he was appointed its general in 1727. Among his first duties was to supervise the certification of Augustine's bones in Pavia. Information was gathered promptly. In February, Benedict received official notice from Ragusa (Dubrovnik) that among the relics held there were indeed the axial vertebrae from Augustine's spine. There were fingers in the Hermit's church of San Agostino in Montalcino, in Piacenza, and in Valencia in Spain. Bellelli arrived in Pavia on April 17, 1728, and stayed until September 22.[4] He wrote up some material for the controversy and then returned to Rome. Later he prepared a new edition of the *Mens,* which was published in Rome in 1737; he subsequently engaged in a controversy over Augustine with his fellow Hermit Lorenzo Berti. Bellelli died in 1742.[5]

There are several important differences between what happened in the summer of 1728 and the controversy following the initial Invention in 1695. This time there were no miracles and no indication of an involvement of the laity in the evaluation process. The clerics who published new arguments were not part of the Pavian community. There was no mention of the spontaneous reverence that had been shown these unauthenticated relics. Publishing about the bones was strictly controlled. The campaign had two distinct audiences: first, the local communities of Pavia and Milan, and second, the intellectuals in Italy and in Europe who were interested in the issue itself and others who studied the ways in which the Catholic Church preserved its traditions and the reputations of its saints. Approximately the same number of books and pamphlets appeared as in the first controversy; most were published between June and September 1728. A new collection of *vota* was gathered, and some of these were also

3. Mario Rosa, "Bellelli, Fulgenzio," in *Dizionario biografico degli italiani,* 7:624–26.

4. Rodolfo Maiocchi and Nazerino Casacca, *Codex diplomaticus Ord. E. S. Augustini Papiae* (Pavia: C. Rossetti, 1905–15), 5:150–67.

5. Arturo Carlo Jemolo, *Il Giansenismo in Italia prima della rivoluzione* (Bari: Laterza, 1928), 141–57.

published independently. One can only guess at the number of copies of each item that appeared, but probably somewhere between six thousand and fifteen thousand items were available in the Pavia-Milan area, and one or perhaps two thousand were printed in Rome and in Venice. A two-volume edition was published in Venice in 1729 which collected a number of the texts from the original controversy and added some of the 1728 material. The audience for this two-volume set was the scholarly community of Catholic Europe.

The whole process went along very quickly once Bellelli arrived at the end of April. On May 19, Bishop Pertusati issued a broadside stating that he would put up with no carping or quibbling; any who complained were threatened with excommunication. On the same day, Giuseppe de Gregorio (Josephus de Gregoriis) and Alosius Bellagente officially reopened the case concerning Augustine's bones. On May 22 it was stated in a letter that the Canons Regular would indeed accept and willingly venerate the bones as being those of Augustine.[6] By the end of May, all the essentials had been presented to Bishop Pertusati. Specialists were consulted. The painter Bernardino Cicessi was called in to see what could be made of the faded and all but ruined picture in the Jesuits' church whose subject was said to be the Translation carried out by Basil and Florentius. On June 18, a Friday, it was announced that all clergy and all confraternities in the city should plan to join the procession to be held by the bishop on the coming Wednesday. On June 20 the last official meeting about the authenticity of the bones was held. And on the twenty-third a procession progressed from the Duomo to San Pietro.[7] A plenary indulgence was granted to all who visited the saint's relics for the next forty days. By compelling all to participate in the ritual, it implied an acceptance of and an obligation to affirm that Augustine's relics had indeed been found.

Several of the new *vota* were published in early July. The official vote was held in the presence of the bishop on the seventh and eighth of July, a Wednesday and Thursday. The decision was unanimous that the bones

6. Fulgenzio Bellelli, *Collectio actorum atque allegatorum quibus ossa sacra Ticini in confessione S.P.C. et anno 1695 reperta esse S. Augustini Hipp. Episcopi et Ecclesiae Doctoris,* 2 vols. (Venice: Sebastiano Coleti, 1729), 1:207–8.

7. The schedule of these events can be found in Angiol-Guglielmo Artegiani, *Della dichiarazione fatta dall'illustrissimo, e reverendissimo monsignor Pertusati, vescovo di Pavia, circa il sacro deposito del p.s. Agostino gloriossissimo dottore di santo chiesa, lettera di ragguaglio* (1728), esp. 12–16.

were those of St. Augustine. On the following Tuesday, the bishop announced that on Friday the sixteenth he would publicly proclaim that the controversy was over, and that on the nineteenth, a *Te Deum* would be sung, and in the evening there would be a light and fireworks display. A Pavian named Toscani who kept a diary from 1721 to 1772, noted the June procession and the festive illumination in July, and knew of the excommunication threat to all who voiced disagreement. Augustine, though, was not an important saint for him; while his diary lists all sorts of saints' feast days, he never mentions Augustine after these two events.[8]

On August 5 a letter came from Rome reminding all concerned that this decision was not to be an occasion for controversy.[9] And, on September 22, Benedict issued a letter confirming the judgment promulgated by Bishop Pertusati on the authenticity of the bones. His letter reviewed the history of the Translations, confirmed the authenticity of the Invention, acknowledged the continued division of the cathedral between the two orders, and included a strong command that any more questioning of this decision would be punished.[10] A major celebration was held from October 10 to 14 (Sunday to Thursday) to commemorate Augustine's first Translation. Sunday began with "universal bell ringing," and a Portuguese princess arrived on the fourteenth to receive the plenary indulgence.[11]

In 1729 the architect Lorenzo Cassani did some redesigning of the choir of San Pietro and may have prepared to do some work on the crypt altar. Perhaps nothing had been done since 1695.[12] There may have been a shortage of funds from Rome for this construction, for nothing seems to have come of it. The next year, 1730, brought a new pope, a Florentine who took the name Clement XII. His secretary of state, Cardinal Giuseppe Firrao, a patron of the Canons Regular, commissioned Filippo Barigioni to prepare a new altar in San Pietro. An immense block of marble was

8. BNPav Mss. Ticinensis 751, "A. Toscani, Diario per gli anni 1721–1772," 10–11.

9. Ibid., 234, "Memorie e pareri."

10. *Bullarum diplomatum et privilegium sanctorum romanorum pontificum* (Turin: Vecco, 1871), 22:710–13 (no. 239). There is an error in the date of the letter: it is given as 1725, but it should be 1728.

11. *Breve relacion de la invencion del sagrafo cuerpo de nuestro gran padre San Agustin, y declaracion de su identidad,* 20 pages.

12. Alida Casale Grande, "Cassani, Lorenzo Bartolomeo," in *Dizionario biografico degli italiani,* 21:438–40.

brought to Pavia, and Barigioni's designs were carved by Giuseppe Giardoni, Antonio Petrocci, and Gaetano Alessandrini. The work was completed in 1738.

Essentially no new facts were added to the controversy in the summer of 1728. Three major new pieces arguing for authenticity were written by Giusto Fontanini, Giuseppe de Gregorio, and Fulgenzio Bellelli. Fontanini authored a piece in Latin and a shorter Italian version, both published in Rome. In the same year Fontanini published his *De corpore sancti Augustini Hipponensis episopi et ecclesiae doctoris ticini reperto in confessione aedis sancti Petri in Coelo aureo disquisitio ubi antiqua ecclesiae disciplina, in tumulando corpore sancti Augustini servata, ex postrema ejus inventione explicatur; quam etiam summorum Pontificum diplomata, Praesulum Ticenensium acta, veterum tabularum atque historicorum fides cumulate confirmant* (Concerning the body of St. Augustine, bishop of Hippo, doctor of the Church, found in the crypt of the Basilica of San Pietro in Ciel d'Oro, an inquiry into where according to ancient Church teaching the body of the saint was preserved in a burial, its Invention is explained; in which the edicts of the papacy, and of the city of Pavia, are confirmed by old archives and historical proofs). It was 120 pages long and contained an index.[13] At the same time an Italian version from the same publisher was issued, *Ragioni per l'identità del corpo di Santo Agostino vescovo d'Ippone e dottor della chiesa scoperto nella confessione della basilica di San Pietro in Caelo aureo di Pavia estratte dalla disquisizione Latina* (Justifications about the identity of the body of St. Augustine, bishop of Hippo and doctor of the Church, discovered in the crypt of the Basilica of San Pietro in Ciel d'Oro, taken from the Latin inquiry); it was sixty pages long. The Latin edition was dedicated to Benedict XIII by Fontanini; the Italian was dedicated to Cardinal Pier Marcellino Corradini by a relative of the publisher, Giambattista Bernabò. The dedication to Benedict is dated January and the approval letters are from April. Benedict had assembled a sophisticated, up-to-date, and learned group of scholars to push through the Augustine issue.

13. It was published by Rocco Bernabò; see 1:269–359 in the two-volume 1729 edition of the *Collectio actorum.* Dario Busolini, "Fontanini, Giusto," in *Dizionario biografico degli italiani,* 48:747–52.

Benedict knew and chose his men well. Early-eighteenth-century Rome understood and presented itself as a modern state; the image of Rome and especially the papacy as a medieval anachronism was a product of the nineteenth century. Benedict and the intellectuals who worked for him saw themselves as world-class scholars, not just in theology but equally up-to-date on the latest developments in the sciences and historical scholarship of both Catholic and Protestant researchers.

At the very beginning of his book Fontanini, makes it clear that in his view the delay in resolving the controversy was the consequence of envy and the rivalry between the two orders, particularly that of the Canons toward the Hermits. But such quarrels should not prevent getting to the truth of the matter. Fontanini reviewed all the forensic and textual evidence familiar from the earlier controversy. He examined the theories on the dating of Augustine's Translations and brought the issue up-to-date with the latest hypotheses, including Leibniz's contribution to the debate as well as that of Edmund Martène; he agreed with their arguments that the date was 722. Fontanini included the list of the bones; he commented on the glass vials, too, noting that they often indicated a martyr's burial, but that the glass should be stained red, though no such color was found here. He composed short essays on some troublesome medieval Latin prepositions and the meaning of certain dialect words describing the crypt altar which had been part of the controversy. And perhaps because he could not think of another place to publish it, he included a final chapter in the Latin edition that considered why Pavia had two names in Latin: Papiam and Ticinum. The Italian edition made his hostility to Montfauçon clear. In his *Diarium,* Montfauçon gave tacit support to the Canons and gave credit to their story that Augustine was buried in Mortara. In this Mabillon showed the greater judgment, according to Fontanini, for from the *Iter* one can see that at least Mabillon knew where to pray to Augustine; he had worshipped at the lamp in the crypt altar.

Another new contribution was published by the Augustinian Hermit Giuseppe de Gregorio. His essay was part of the case that Bellelli was putting together in Pavia for Bishop Pertusati. Gregorio published a thirty-eight-page Latin pamphlet titled *In causa identitates corporis S. Augustini, Hipponensis Episopi, & Ecclesiae doctoris eximi, quod inventum fuit sub die prima octobris 1695* (Concerning the case of the identity of the body of St. Augustine, bishop of Hippo & an outstanding doctor of the Church, which was found [Invented] on the first day of October, 1695). The work was dedicated to Bishop Pertusati and later expanded for inclusion in the 1729 *Collectio.*[14] Gregorio gave special attention to the letters exchanged between the papacy and San Pietro. Knowing that Pope Benedict was personally interested, he went out of his way to include an account of the 1698 discovery of the apostle Bartholomew in Benevento; this Invention had been one of the more spectacular religious events that occurred when Orsini, now Benedict XIII, was archbishop there. Bellelli wrote his own account about the authenticity of the bones; it was written in Italian, and in the two-volume edition it followed right after Gregorio's essay.[15] It was titled *Alcune considerazioni sopra la causa pendente avanti Monsignor Illustrissimo e reverendissimo Vescovo di Pavia circa l'identità del corpo del Padre Sant'Agostino* (Some considerations concerning the case pending before the Most Reverend Bishop of Pavia concerning the identity of the body of St. Augustine). Bellelli had issued this pamphlet of twenty unnumbered pages in June, and it was published in Pavia by Giovanni Antonio Ghidini. He had not signed his name as author but simply called himself "un religioso Agostiniano" (an Augustinian Hermit).

There must have been an interest in this pamphlet, because it was promptly reprinted in Venice by Biagio Madura; reprints had not appeared in the earlier controversy. But there is more to it than this: along with the pamphlet the Venetian printer included another essay of Bellelli's that had been published in late July or early August, *Altre poche considerazioni aggiunte alle prime già date in luce sopra la causa pendente avanti Monsi. illustrissimo e reverendissimo vescovo di Pavia circa l'identità del corpo di S. Agostino fatta da un religioso agostiniano* (A couple of other observations concerning the case pending before the Most Reverend Bishop of Pavia concerning the identity of St. Augustine's body). As Bellelli explained, he had written *Alcune considerazioni* to put to rest the accusations and arguments made by Mario Callini a quarter of a century earlier. But then someone had published an attack on the identity of the bones in late June or early July, restating all the old arguments that had left the issue in doubt at the beginning of the century. Bellelli referred to the pamphlet by an Italian title, *Annotazioni;* it may have appeared in Italian, though the only version I have found has the Latin title *Adnotationes super iis quae huc usque alata sunt pro identitate sacrorum ossium repertorum in confessorio S. Petri in*

14. Ibid., 1:360–436.

15. Ibid., 1:437–72.

Coelo aureo Papiae de anno 1695 cum veris reliquiis eximii ecclesiae doctoris S. Patris Augustini (Annotations concerning that which has just been alleged concerning the sacred bones found in the crypt of San Pietro in Ciel d'Oro in Pavia in 1695 as the true relics of the outstanding Doctor of the Church St. Augustine). The *Adnotationes* was a pamphlet of six unnumbered pages which gave no indication of the author or information about its publication. The author had seen Fontanini's book, and was in part answering it. He wrote to support the position taken by Callini; his conclusion was that no new argument or decisive evidence had been furnished to justify any positive identification of the relics.

Given that the pope's attention was focused on Pavia, and with all the concern about Augustine's bones, the author and printer were extremely bold to publish this work. The Venetian publisher's decision to reprint both of Bellelli's pamphlets represented a different kind of boldness: here was a completely legitimate way of presenting the opposition's view about the relics, and it conformed with Benedict's directives that there be no controversy. Scarcely anyone would have had access to or remembered the old works of Callini and Bellini. A context for the controversy was needed. It would not have been safe to print the *Adnotationes* even in Venice, and it may even have been impossible to get a copy, but no one could object to Madura's printing Bellelli; and Bellelli's second text, honest to a fault, made explicit all of the objections posed by his adversaries as well as his refutation of them.

A couple of manuscript documents hostile to the identification of the relics as those of Augustine seem to have been prepared around this same time. One titled "Resultato del Congre. sú la cause di S. Agustino" (Conclusions of the meeting about the case of St. Augustine), in twelve unnumbered pages, reviewed the various controversial points and noted how they were answered. A second manuscript has also survived; the author claims that a delay was needed to investigate all the evidence thoroughly. This is a manuscript of four unnumbered pages, titled "Nella discussione che occorrà da farsi sopra qualche reiliguia si devono notare" (Some points that ought to be noticed about the discussion that took place about some relics).[16] Clearly the defenders of the Canons did not simply concede in silence.

16. Both documents appear in a manuscript titled "Memorie e pareri," BNPav Mss. Ticinensis 234.

In early July, Giuseppe Antonio Sassi (Sax), the head librarian of the Ambrosiana in Milan, published a pamphlet of fourteen unnumbered pages in the guise of a letter addressed to Bishop Pertusati, *Epistola apologetica pro identitate corporis S. Augustini* (A letter arguing about the identity of the body of St. Augustine). Sassi may have been responding to the *Adnotationes;* certainly he attacked the position of Callini. Sassi, following the ecclesiastical winds of fortune, had written a letter in 1727 defending the discovery of the apostle Bartholomew in Benevento.[17] The *Epistola* appears to have been published in Milan, perhaps by Gaspare Tedeschi: he is listed as the bookseller. Toward the end of July the Augustinian Hermit Angiol-Guglielmo Artegiani published an eighteen-page pamphlet, probably in Pavia, titled *Della dichiarazione fatta dall'illustrissio, e reverendissimo Monsignor Pertusati vescovo di Pavia, circa il sacro deposito del P. S. Agostino* (About the statement made by Bishop Pertusati of Pavia concerning the sacred remains of St. Augustine). Artegiani also appeared to be reacting to the *Adnotationes,* though his stated adversary was Callini. Artegiani speculated that Bellini was in fact Callini; the information about Trevisan's authorship revealed in 1710 by the *Giornale* had apparently been forgotten.[18] While Artegiani also reviewed the main arguments in the controversy, he devoted a great deal of space to describing the celebrations attendant on the bishop's authentication of the relics. His letter was included in the first volume of the *Collectio actorum.*

Sometime in 1728, presumably in the summer, a rather different sort of work appeared in Milan published by Carlo Bolzani. This was a broadside that contains twenty-four little images surrounding a picture of St. Augustine, who is holding a copy of the Rule of the Augustinian Hermits. Underneath all the pictures is an image of the silver box with the Lombard cross in which were found Augustine's bones. Most of the images are scenes from Augustine's life, with special emphasis given to his role as founder of the Hermits. The last five concern his two Translations and representations of miracles attributed to him. The work concludes with the 1695 Invention. The use of pictorial representation

17. Giuseppe Antonio Sassi, "Ragione per provare l'esistenza del corpo di S. Bartolomeo in Benevento esposte in una lettere alla Santità Benedetto XIII," in *Raccolta d'opuscoli scientifici e filologici* 15 (1743), art. 3. The letter is dated March 1, 1727.

18. Knowledge of the review had not disappeared for it was cited for a different purpose; see Bellelli, *Collectio actorum,* 2:140.

alone to represent the story of Augustine was a new addition to the controversy.

There was international interest in this event. In Spain, Augustin Antonio Minuart wrote about Augustine's bones in the *Breve resumen de todo lo que conduce a la mayor declaracion* . . . (A brief summary of everything that led to this declaration . . .), which was published in Barcelona in 1728; in Madrid in 1728, Juan C. Elacurriaga wrote *De la invención y declaración de N.P.S Augustin* (The Invention and announcement concerning St. Augustine). These simply retell the story based on the Italian and Latin works and documents about the matter. Another volume similar in content was published in Leipzig in 1728, edited by G. F. Jenichen, titled *De reliquiis divi Augustini* (Concerning the relics of St. Augustine), which reprinted in Latin several of the essays on the authenticity of the bones. The first publication to describe the event without taking part in the controversy or simply repeating its contents appeared in a history of Benedict's pontificate published in 1731.[19]

The most comprehensive collection was the two-volume editions published in Venice, the *Collectio actorum atque allegatorum quibus ossa sacra Ticini in confessione. . . .* These volumes contain some of the official letters, documents, and texts of many of the items previously published concerning the controversy. The only major item not included was Beretti's *Lynchnus,* perhaps because of its length. Giusto Fontanini was appointed to handle the big summary document that was to be issued in Rome and then in Venice. Fontanini had made his name at the beginning of the eighteenth century with his defense of Mabillon's *De re diplomatica* against the Jesuit Germon.[20] He had been identified with Benedetto Bacchini and was a friend of Muratori. But Muratori and Fontanini came to quarrel. The controversy concerned a territorial dispute between Modena and Rome over who had political authority over the Comacchio, a marshy region near the Adriatic on the border of the papal territories and those of Ferrara. Fontanini had been given the job of defending the claims of the papacy; Muratori argued on behalf of the Este family of Ferrarra, his patrons. The Comacchio controversy embittered his relations with Fontanini, and per-

19. *Das Ruhm- und Wunderwürdige Leben und Thaten Pabsts Benedicti,* 158–61.

20. On the controversy, see Carlo Corsetti, *Guerre diplomatiche e storiografia moderne* (Rome: Aracne, 1992). Scipione Maffei was also a supporter; see Maffei's journal *Osservazioni letterarie che possono servir di continuazone al Giornale de'Letterati d'Italia* 2 (1738), arts. 7 and 8.

haps it was inevitable that even before *De ingeniorum moderatione* found a publisher, Fontanini was preparing his refutation of it.[21]

Fontanini's use of the publishing conventions of his day suggests that something rather different was going on with Augustine volumes published in Rome and the legal process being enacted in Pavia. Fontanini's direct contribution to the 1728 debate was his *De corpore sancti Augustini* (Concerning the body of St. Augustine). The book's official approvers tell a curious story. The approval letters, which confirmed the book's orthodoxy, were written by Francesco Bianchini and Celestino Galiani. Bianchini was from Verona and had learned his theology and historical method from Enrico Noris. Noris's work on Augustine had been condemned by the Spanish Index as being Jansenist, though his orthodoxy had been affirmed by Rome. Noris also had had serious disagreements with Mabillon, and his student Bianchini was on certain matters hostile to Mabillon's influence.[22] Bianchini had earned an international reputation with his 1697 work *La storia universale,* which had used the artifacts, coins, statues, and inscriptions of antiquity to show how visual evidence, the material productions of a culture, could be used to reconstruct archaic history. Later, in Rome, he became an important popularizer of Newton's ideas. Bianchini had preached the sermon on the papal election for the conclave that elevated Benedict XIII. His fellow approver was Celestino Galiani, a Neapolitan and another promoter of the ideas of Newton and of John Locke.[23] In the early 1730s, Galiani in Naples was a co-founder of a scientific academy that promoted Newton's work. He had a run-in with the Inquisition when Locke's *Essay Concerning Human Understanding* was placed on the Index in 1734. Later, he was the royal chaplain for Carlo III, king of Naples, and was instrumental in pushing through the decision to allow Jews to reside legally in Naples—though this decree was rescinded a couple of years later owing to public pressure. The approvers of this book claiming the

21. Sergio Bertelli, *Erudizione e storia in Ludovico Antonio Muratori* (Naples: Istituto Italiano per gli Studi Storici, 1960), chap. 2, 100–174.

22. Arnaldo Momigliano, "Mabillon's Italian Disciples," in *Essays in Historiography* (Oxford: Blackwell, 1977), 282–85.

23. Celestino Galiani is the central figure of Vincenzo Ferrone's *Scienza natura religione: mondo Newtonismo e cultura italiana nel primo settecento* (Naples: Jovene, 1982); in English, *The Intellectual Roots of the Italian Enlightenment: Newtonian Science, Religion, and Politics in the Early Eighteenth Century,* trans. Sue Brotherton (Atlantic Highlands, N.J.: Humanities Press, 1995). For the 1720s, see chap. 6.

authenticity of Augustine's bones were thus two men whose intellectual commitments placed them among the foremost proponents of Newtonian thought in Italy. This suggests that there was some kind of official approval at Benedict's court for Newtonian science. We do know that Bianchini and Galiani had reached the conclusion that Newtonianism had more to offer Catholic orthodoxy than the approaches of either Descartes or the descendants of Aristotle. Fontanini appears to have been tacitly linking himself to their position; this kind of evidence makes one wonder what else might have come from Rome if Benedict's pontificate had continued for a longer time. For most Pavians, the names Galiani and Bianchini would have meant nothing. A Roman or perhaps a Neapolitan might have been curious to learn what kind of material these arch-Newtonians were approving, but for a Pavian, the interest of the book would have been the issue of Augustine's relics.

A curious manuscript document related to the 1729 publication was prepared and has been preserved in Venice. It is a collection of manuscript copies, broadsides, and pamphlets related to the 1728 controversy.[24] Although it contains some of the material that was printed in the 1729 Venetian edition, there are differences in content. It seems to have been assembled by a reader who wanted his own collection of documents related to the controversy. While absence of evidence is a weak argument, nothing of a similar sort seems to have been done in Pavia. This Venetian reader had more of an interest in preserving the Pavian quarrel than anyone in Pavia.

The most original reconsideration of the issue of the bones was written by Ludovico Muratori.[25] Despite the thoughtfulness of his argument and its lucidity, it did not bring about a change in the 1728 decision. Nor did subsequent surveys of the evidence by competent judges result in recommendations that support Muratori's position. Muratori had visited Augustine's tomb in September 1714. In 1728, Muratori was fifty-six and in the middle of some of the projects for which he earned the reputation of be-

24. Biblioteca Marciana di Venezia, Mss. It. V. 58 (5820) "Atti della causa sopra l'identità del corpo di S. Agostino in Pavia."

25. Sergio Bertelli, *Erudizione e storia in Ludovico Antonio Muratori.* Bruno Neveu, "Muratori et l'historographie gallicane," in *Érudition et religion aux XVIIe et XVIIIe siècles* (Paris: Albin Michel, 1994), 105–74.

ing one of the greatest historians in an age of great historians. Muratori was remarkably prolific, often simultaneously producing folio volumes bulging with erudition, along with polemical tracts about conflicts taking place in the contemporary Italian political and cultural scene, as well as essays on Catholic spirituality. Besides being a master of the arts of historical erudition, he was renowned as a literary theorist, dabbled in the natural sciences, and made substantial contributions to the theological discourse of his age.

Muratori had a sincere interest in St. Augustine, in both his writings and his relics. In 1695, when in Milan, he had inquired into the initial Invention, and was relieved when it seemed as if nothing further was going to come of the matter. In 1705 he wrote a long introduction, *Prolegomena,* to Celso Cerri's *Elucidatio augustinianae de divina gratia doctrinae* (An Augustinian explanation of the teaching about divine grace); its supposed place of publication was Cologne. The primary purpose of this work was to answer the charges made by Jean LeClerc in his 1703 *Appendix augustiniana.* After further reflection, Muratori took up this issue again in his *De ingeniorum moderatione in religionis negotio* (Concerning the moderation of our cleverness in religious matters), a book he completed in 1708, but he had difficulty printing it in Italy; it appeared in 1714, published, it was said, in Paris under his publicly known Arcadian pseudonym of Lamindi Pritanii. This work, among other things, presented his view that free scientific and historical inquiry did not threaten the values and beliefs of orthodox religion; the unprejudiced investigation in pursuit of the truth was the best defense of the Catholic faith.

In the beginning of the eighteenth century, he had been involved in the controversy over Mabillon's work and the place of erudite studies in the religious life. At this time he and his teacher Benedetto Bacchini were aided by Giusto Fontanini; but, as noted, this friendship collapsed over a quarrel as to who had political authority over the Comacchio.

Muratori's research involved him deeply in the medieval period. One scholarly consequence of the Comacchio fight was his decision to prepare *Delle antichità estensi* (Concerning the origins of the Este family), a pioneering study into the beginning of the Italian Middle Ages. This topic was directly related to a parallel project being pursued by Leibniz into the origins of the House of Brunswick; the two exchanged numerous letters as both sought to identify an unambiguous beginning point for the families of their noble patrons. For Muratori this served as a preliminary test or first fruit of his subsequent work; for Leibniz it was the coda to a diverse and productive career. Volume one of the Este family project appeared in 1717, shortly after Leibniz's death in November of the previous year; volume two appeared much later, in 1740. Muratori conceived, outlined, and began work on a vast project to publish the major primary documents of the Italian medieval period, a work known as the *Rerum Italicarum scriptores.* Twenty-four folio volumes appeared between 1724 and 1738; volume twenty-five, containing indices, appeared posthumously in 1751. Such investigations into the origins of the contemporary political scene in Italy were bound to cause controversy, and his first volume almost did not get published because of opposition from Rome.[26] His work on the first volumes put him in contact with the new librarian of the Ambrosiana in Milan, Giuseppe Sassi. Muratori found Sassi's slow response to his manuscript queries vexing. Giovanni Gaspare Beretti transcribed for him the *De laudibus civitatis ticinensis* and sent it on to Muratori in September 1721. Beretti had participated in the original controversy concerning the bones, but not in the second; Sassi himself had contributed an essay in 1728.

From 1732 to 1738, Muratori completed his *Antiquitates italicae medii aevi* (Antiquities or the cultural and social history of the Italian Middle Ages), a six-volume collection of seventy-five dissertations on all aspects of medieval history. These essays demonstrated that cultural history, or "philosophical history," as the eighteenth century called it, could also be written by the erudite and be firmly grounded in a thorough study and mastery of the evidence. Some of his thoughts on the Augustine Invention appeared in Dissertation 58, *De christianorum veneratione erga sanctos post declinationem romani imperii* (Concerning the veneration of Christian saints after the fall of the Roman Empire). After the labors of gathering the *Rerum,* and the diachronic analysis required to prepare the essays of the *Antiquitates,* Muratori undertook his last great project, the *Annali d'Italia,* a synchronic history of the Italian world from A.D. 1 to 1749.

Muratori's *Annali* was not a history of Italy arranged by significant periods and developments using overlapping chronologies to structure and present a composite picture of an era; it was a year-by-year account of what happened in each year. Such an order of presentation is almost as

26. Sergio Bertelli, *Erudizione e storia in Ludovico Antonio Muratori* (Naples: Istituto italiano per gli Studi Storici in Napoli, 1960), 281–90.

foreign to our habits of thought as the *Acta sanctorum,* which took up the lives of the saints according to their feast dates in the annual calendar. In certain respects Muratori's order of presentation imitated Mabillon's *Annales* of the Benedictine order. But the more direct precedent was the *Annales* of Cardinal Baronio, and it was to correct the bias and errors of his work that Muratori composed his own. Muratori had another more fundamental and straightforward aim: to clarify Italy's complex past. His *Rerum* had made possible the study of the Italian Middle Ages, and similar projects in France and Germany had opened up these regions as areas of historical study as well. The *Annali* and the *Antiquitates* showed what could be done with this evidence.

At this time, "medieval" or "Middle Ages" had not yet become a widely used term for a specific historical period. And the name did not have negative connotations. To be sure, certain Italian Humanists of the fourteenth and fifteenth centuries committed to the revival of the learning of antiquity disparaged the learning and the Latinity of the intervening—the middle or medieval—period which preceded their own. Their focus had been on the decline of classical Latin, which was restored in their own time. The term "Middle Ages" as a description of a distinct historical period from the fall of Rome to the fifteenth century received a broader usage with certain authors in the late seventeenth century. The Dutch religious historian Georg Horn adopted it in 1666 to describe a period of Church history; Paul Hachenberg used the term in the title of his 1675 *Germania media.* He died in 1681 at the age of twenty-nine, but his book was published again in 1686 and 1709. In 1688, Christoph Cellarius used the term as a description of a period of secular history. But "the Middle Ages" only became a term commonly used by European historians in the early nineteenth century; neither Gibbon, Voltaire, or Montesquieu adopted it.[27]

It was clear by the 1740s that the consequence of making available all this new evidence was not a deepened understanding of how modern Europe arose from this past, but the belief that if Europe was ever to be truly "modern," it needed to break away from this past. Muratori rejected the

27. Eugenio Dupré-Theseider, "Sull'uso del termine 'Medioevo' presso il Muratori," in *Miscellanea di studi muratoriani* (Modena: Storia Patria per le Antiche Provincie Modensi, 1951), 418–34. On Muratori as a medievalist, see Giovanni Tabacco, "Muratori medievista," *Rivista storica italiana* 85 (1973), 200–16; Bertelli, *Erudizione e storia in Ludovico Muratori,* 445–53; and Giuseppe Giarizzo, "Alle origini della medievistica moderna (Vico, Giannone, Muratori)," *Bollettino dell'Istituto storico italiano per il medioevo* 74 (1962), 35–86.

view that the way for the modern age to define itself was to accept a version of European history that began with a period of high culture in pagan antiquity followed by centuries of monkish dullness whose accomplishments, if any, could be safely ignored by the vital intelligence and spirit of the mid-eighteenth century. Mabillon, Muratori, and their followers understood that certain patterns of thought and values in this "middle" period were different from their own. They also recognized that evaluating this previous time as if its records and documents had been prepared by men of unparalleled virtue and wisdom would be as unproductive as regarding them as written by the ignorant dupes of clever priests or politicians. They took inspiration from the scholarship on republican and imperial Rome written in the seventeenth and eighteenth centuries which had begun to understand the ancient Romans as people, not simply as either foolish pagans or paragons of virtue. Mabillon's followers had hoped that the same treatment might be applied to Europe's medieval period. Vico had outlined in his *New Science* a way of synthesizing research on the Middle Ages with that of Homeric Greece and archaic Rome. Muratori, following his own method, sought to do the same for Italian history.

The narrative history of western Europe—starting with the accomplishments of the Greek and Roman pagans, then a fall into a medieval darkness followed by the light of modernity—even if untrue, had all the essentials of a good story and explained, or at least made intelligible, a confused record of events. It gave a clear purpose and direction to modern history beyond the ambiguous outline found in New Testament texts about the Second Coming. The early eighteenth century was a time when finding a direction, discerning the moral purpose of European history, was of particular importance to certain European intellectuals. Muratori may not have read Vico's *Scienza nuova,* but he had seen his 1728 autobiography. Vico's response to this desire for a new paradigm or pattern of historical change was clearly stated in both works. Muratori, and, one may suspect, Vico himself, failed to grasp fully the implications of the kind of cultural history outlined in *Scienza nuova.* Vico regarded the medieval period as similar to what he called the Age of Gods and Heroes in remote antiquity. To Vico's mind this would have been high praise, and one of the great challenges to the historical imagination was the attempt to study these prerational periods of human history. But the far more common reaction to the genuine difficulties of understanding these preceding ages was to see them as failed or ignorant cultures. The method of Mabillon had produced remarkable amounts of new information, but its consequence seemed to be the dismissal or devaluation of the very histories it was designed to study. Instead of increasing understanding, the initial reaction to all this new information was to reject it. Montesquieu's *De l'esprit des lois* was a partial exception, for in it Montesqiueu used the evidence of medieval law and legal procedures to explain the role of the nobility in French society of his day. He contrasted his method with what he regarded as the unhistorical and rival theses of Boulainvillier and DuBois. Montesquieu saw little that was positive in the contributions of ecclesiastics, and concentrated his effort on demonstrating the vitality and intelligence of the judicial practices of the Middle Ages. Muratori would have rejected that assessment.

Muratori was particularly worried about the shoddy use of historical evidence involving ecclesiastical matters, and the tendency to interpret the past in light of the interests of particular influential groups. If these abuses were not corrected, he feared that the trust in and respect for honest historical research would also be undermined. The time period in which frauds were most likely and had the most to gain from the powerful interests involved was from A.D. 250 to around 1450. Keeping this era a time of darkness and confusion suited certain families and political bodies. Claims about the origins of noble families, the foundation of religious orders and other ecclesiastical establishments, customs, traditions, and laws, the understanding of private property, even the foundation of political institutions and the authority of kings themselves could be undermined by too much impartial historical research. Given what was at stake, it is not surprising that some looked for other solutions. Bianchini and Galiani (and perhaps Fontanini saw the wisdom in this) had turned from Mabillon's historical science to the other great intellectual revolution of the 1680s, the mathematical physics of Newton, as a better support for Catholic orthodoxy than historical research. But this avenue was effectively closed in the mid-1730s with the condemnation of Locke by the Roman Index. Newton's science seemed off-limits until the Jesuit Boscovich at mid-century showed a way around its supposed materialism. But the conjunction of possibility suggested in the late 1720s could not be recreated. There was no movement, after the turn to Newton proved unacceptable, to return to Muratori's advice and follow the French and Mabillon. The Neapolitan Vico had come up with a solution of his own, but few understood the suggestions of his *New Science.* Naples's other great historical thinker, Pietro

Giannone, had started writing a book on these very issues, *Il triregno,* but his life imprisonment in 1735 effectively silenced his potential contribution.

Muratori's work on the Invention of Augustine's bones was part of his general campaign to preserve a serious concern for the Middle Ages among nonspecialist readers. The circumstances of its publication gave him little cause to be optimistic about the future of independent historical research on ecclesiastical subjects. The first edition of *Motivi di credere tuttavia ascoso e non iscoperto in Pavia l'anno MDCXCV, il sacro corpo Santo Agostino dottore della chiesa . . . in risposta alle scritture pubblicate questo anno 1728 in favore dell'identità di esso corpo* (Reasons to believe that the holy body of St. Augustine, doctor of the Church, is still concealed and not found in Pavia . . . in response to the works published in this year, 1728, in favor of this identification of the body) seems to have appeared in 1728; at least the title makes that claim. The ninety-two-page work lists no publishing information; it contains forty-eight chapters. This edition includes a note at the end signed by Tommaso Alfano, a Dominican, who was a promoter of erudite antiquarian studies and the modern science of the Cartesians.[28] Alfano was in Naples in 1728, and the work may have been printed there. There is a printer's mark of a female nude holding a flower, standing in a bay with sails visible in the distance: this might be a representation of the Siren Parthenope, the legendary founder of Naples; the sail would be that of Odysseus. Muratori's nephew Proposto Soli Muratori was in contact with Mosca, who was publishing translations of Newtonian writings in Naples during these years. The note at the end of the 1760 Naples edition suggests that this had in fact occurred. An edition also appeared in 1730 claiming to be published in Trent, but in fact it was printed in Lucca; it was the same text, but a change in format made it 120 pages. It contains no mention of the author; an unsigned note by the printer explains that it was published so as not to deprive readers of an interesting controversy.

28. Fausto Nicolini, "Alfano, Tommaso Maria," in *Dizionario biografico degli Italiani,* 2: 260–61. Alfano's press republished this note in 1760 in his *Raccolta delle opere minori di Ludovico Antonio Muratori* (Naples: T. Alfano and G. Ponzelli, 1757–64), 10:1–92. It has the same pagination and format as the original edition. Dario Busolini, "Fontanini, Giusto," in *Dizionario biografico degli italiani,* 48:747–52. Fontanini responded to Muratori with "Inventario delle Imposture Contenute nel Libello de'Motivi Contro l'Identita del Corpo di S. Agostino." It was never published and seems to have had little circulation.

Muratori did not promote or advertise his role as the author of the *Motivi* at the time. In a letter of February 1731 to Francesco Brembati of Bergamo, he briefly discussed the 1728 controversy and mentioned the *Motivi* but did not claim authorship of the work.[29] In his 1738 volume of the *Antiquitates,* which contained Dissertation 58, discussing the theft of relics, he acknowledged his authorship.[30]

In the *Motivi,* Muratori explained that his primary purpose was to answer Fontanini's Roman edition of *De corpore* and his Milanese *In causa identitatis.* Muratori attacked Fontanini's arguments; nothing indicated that he saw his role, as had the Venetian journalists in 1710, as one of trying to restrain and correct Rome or the pope. Muratori's first complaint was that, given the importance of the issues, the fact that only a couple of months had been allowed for the investigation was a serious error of procedure. He began by berating his opponent Fontanini for wasting the reader's time with a vain display of erudition on matters that no one disputed. Why go over the evidence concerning the Liutprand Translation, especially when he had nothing to add and left the reader no wiser than before? Fontanini, in his view, had been satisfied with simply arguing that since these bones could be, indeed ought to be, those of St. Augustine, why not identify them as such? Of course, they could be his bones, granted Muratori, but was it likely that they were? Muratori spent much of his argument describing the norms of tomb decoration and the lengths to which people had gone to conceal relics in the medieval period. He explained the differences between contemporary and earlier customs of burying the dead. He repeated the problems of interpreting the significance of what few bones remained as well as the ones that were not there; he also agreed with those who thought that the erased name on the box was poor evidence. In other parallel cases, the name of the person buried had been engraved in the nearby stone. And the absence of the designation "saint" was also very odd. If these bones were those of Augustine, it would mean that the evidence that remained was contrary to the practices and rituals followed at the time when Augustine's body was known to have been translated to Pavia.

Muratori reviewed all the earlier textual documentation, reiterating the

29. Ludovico Muratori, *Carteggio a Francesco Brembati* (February 6, 1731), no. 2998 (Florence: Olschki, 1975–), 7:2961.

30. Ludovico Muratori, *Opere* (Venice: Antonio Curti & Giacomo, 1790), 47:17.

difficulties of making coherent sense of the diverse statements. From the beginning it was not known where in San Pietro Liutprand had placed Augustine's remains. And, he observed, papal letters had no special authority about matters of fact on which they had no direct information. It was clear that the popes had been responding to local pleas and that their repetition or use of certain prepositions indicating the location of Augustine's body was not based on personal knowledge of where the body lay. Furthermore, he observed, San Pietro had apparently been founded before Liutprand arrived with the body. Some relics, now unknown, must have been part of the original founding. Since the crypt altar would be a usual place for such relics, how could one be sure that the 1695 Invention was not of the bones of San Pietro's first holy relics?

Muratori reviewed some of the history of the thefts of sacred relics and what had typically been done to prevent them. He mentioned the case of Pavia's own San Epifanio and the martyr San Vito, whose bodies were hidden during the wars between Milan and Pavia in the fourteenth century. This would have been the most reasonable time for the supposed Translation carried out by Basil and Florentius. To prevent abduction, the relics of San Epifanio had been placed five feet underground, directly under a wall. Yet his body was found, stolen, and transported to Hildesheim.[31] Certainly a relic as prestigious as that of Augustine would have received at least comparable treatment. We know it was not found. Would it have gone unnoticed if it were located in such an obvious place as under the floor behind the crypt altar? Furthermore, Muratori noted, the burial places of Milanese saints in the 830s were given lavish treatment. This was only a century after Augustine's Translation to Pavia. Was there any reason to believe that taste and custom had changed so much in a hundred years? Another piece of cultural evidence came from England, where in 1091 it was thought necessary to hide the body of St. Augustine of Canterbury out of fear of the Normans. The location of the body was forgotten; his Invention was brought about by a revelation, but positive identification was possible because of the carved inscriptions found with the body. Wasn't it likely that a similar thing would have been done for St. Augustine in Pavia? Also, Muratori observed, the Portuguese Crown wrote a letter in 1575 to the Cathedral of San Pietro explaining their interest in setting up twelve lamps to burn perpetually before Augustine's relics. The

31. This theft is described in the *Acta sanctorum* (January 1858), 1:257 (January 5).

reason they later scaled back their offer from twelve lamps to only one, he suggested, was that they had learned that the precise location of the relics was unknown. Muratori concluded that the preponderance of the evidence supported the claim that the relics were those of some unknown martyr, nothing more.

Muratori wrote his essay in Italian, one presumes, because he wanted to make his work available to a wide audience that would include the nonspecialist. His primary motivation appears to have been the desire to do the historian's job of preserving the memory of historical narratives and analyses and not to let it be tacitly replaced by a simplified or falsified official story. Muratori presented an argument based on local evidence and supplemented it with a comparative study of similar events from other regions of Europe. Since he did not consider the quarrel between the orders a serious factor in the analysis of the historical facts, his approach did not involve this aspect of the local quarrel. We do not know the extent of the readership of the *Motivi* in Pavia. Presumably someone at this time prepared a manuscript copy of the work.[32]

In the end, the debate between Muratori and Fontanini leaves us in an unexpected position. Muratori's argument, for all his concern with the facts and with the historical reconstruction of the past, is more remote in some ways from our sensibilities than the position taken by Fontanini and Pope Benedict. Muratori's final appeal to Pavia's bishop and to the city was that affirming the Invention would be unworthy of St. Augustine and of the Pavians who long ago thought it right and proper to hide the saint's relics in a very safe place. Instead, Pavians should continue to worship Augustine's bones even though their location in San Pietro was uncertain. Benedict and Fontanini took the less prudent position that local knowledge was knowledge, and it was knowledge *about* something. They placed greater emphasis on the meaning these bones had for the communities involved with San Pietro and their traditions about the location of them. They were also convinced that Rome's judicial procedures guaranteed that they were doing more than simply affirming that the local view was true. We too now tend to favor local testimony and look askance at positions that claim to take an objective viewpoint but whose consequence runs counter to the emphatic beliefs of local, uneducated, but sincere believers. It is also curious to reflect that in 1728 the papacy was cooperating with

32. *Mss. Ticinensis* 428.

individuals who were linked to the projects of Newton and Locke in opposition to Muratori, whose intellectual alliances were with French scholarship and Descartes's science. Both positions took extremely seriously the truths of Catholicism and the values of tradition.

There is no indication that there was a popular audience in Pavia for any of the 1728 controversy or that authors interacted with the concerns and questions of the laity. The authors were responding solely to other printed works. Furthermore, they were not members of the Pavian community but churchmen whose reputations had been made elsewhere. Most of those who had been involved in the 1695 Invention were probably dead by now; in any event, their experience was not appealed too, nor were any still living reexamined in new interviews. Even Beretti was not asked to prepare a new *votum.* None of this proves that the Pavians did not respond to this renewal of the debate about St. Augustine's bones. But the controversy itself was conducted as if no such response existed. The authentication of the bones was handled by Rome; the Pavians appear to have been largely passive in this process, though arguments such as that of Muratori proceeded as if the Pavian bishop still had a voice in the matter. The aim of Fontanini and Bellelli was to establish the appearance of unity and consensus. The primary purpose of the publications was not to persuade but to proclaim conclusions. The 1728 controversy did not seek the involvement of the Pavian laity. Although we do not know for certain, many Pavians may have thought that Rome was finally giving official approval of what they had known to be the truth since 1695.

The 1728 controversy was reviewed in the Leipzig journal *Acta eruditorum*, the most prestigious Protestant book review. In the February 1731 edition the editors reviewed Fontanini's *De corpore S. Augustini;* they presented it in a sympathetic light, hinting that they understood his situation: Benedict XIII had forced Fontanini to write this piece.[33] The editors noted his praise of Beretti and Colli and showed their respect for the learning and vision contained in this little work. In May 1731 the *Acta* reviewed the 1729 Venice *Collectio actorum.*[34] The review began by retelling the history of the controversy, though this time no mention was made of Beretti. It listed

33. *Acta eruditorum* (February 1731), 91–93.

34. Ibid. (May 1731), 215–20.

the contents of each section of the work. But its conclusion was to support the doubts raised by Bellini. The reviewer professed amazement that such intelligent men as Sassi and Fontanini were willing to accommodate themselves to such vulgar fantasies. Instead of echoing the opinion of the *Giornale* of the first controversy—that it was a quarrel between orders—the *Acta* saw the publication as a caving-in to the desires of the uneducated.

The review concluded with a quotation from Cicero's *De finibus* (2.24.77): "Are you ever going to say what you think, or will you change your opinions as you do your clothing, having one outfit for home and another for being in public?" The editors of the *Acta* accused Rome of dealing in some sort of double truth in the style of the Averroists, who were believed to have an orthodox version of their teaching available for popular consumption and another secret teaching for the learned. This attitude marked a change in tone from the days of the journal's more ecumenical beginnings in the 1680s. Instead of attempting a sympathetic understanding of Catholic ecclesiastical scholarship, the reviewer had accepted the caricature of Roman Catholicism as essentially a trick perpetrated by conniving priests. Catholic religious leaders were presumed to be engaged in a form of euhemerism, which fraudulently attributed divine powers to mere mortals. There is no indication that the reviewers had seen Muratori's contribution to this controversy, nor did they review it at a later date. This was probably due not to lack of interest in the issue but to the genuine difficulty for an interested reader remote from the local scene in obtaining an anonymous item or one in which the place of publication was concealed or falsified. Muratori was a respected scholar even among the Lutherans, but their attitude was no longer that exemplified by Bayle of scholarly interest in other religious confessions.

FIVE
Putting the Bones to Rest

RIGHT after Giusto Fontanini finished the volumes justifying the case that the bones found in San Pietro were Augustine's, he took up a new book project that focused on Benedict XIII's well-known enthusiasm for the cult of the saints. Fontanini had done much of the research on the ritual of sanctification as part of a previous book on St. Peter Orseolo, a tenth-century Venetian who was the Doge of Venice before retiring to a monastery. Orseolo's predecessor as Doge had attempted to set himself up as a king and plotted to subvert the aristocratic republic. The saint may have had a hand in the conspiracy that overthrew him. Orseolo's career raised a number of vital issues concerning Venetian church-state relations. For Rome, it was important that the Vatican authorize his sanctification; the Venetian Republic might have made Mark its own, but the other saints of the Veneto were subject to the authority of Peter and of Rome.

Fontanini's new work was titled *Codex constitutionum quas summi, pontifices ediderunt in solemni canonizatione sanctorum* (A collection of the documents on the canonization of saints issued by all the popes); it was published in Rome in 1729. This was a work on the history of the papal canonization of saints, beginning with John XV's 993 canonization of Ulrich, a bishop of Augsburg who died in 973, the first canonization for which the papal bull is extant. The formal process of canonization became fairly standardized during the pontificate of Alexander III in the last part of the twelfth century. Fontanini's book brought the story down to Benedict's 1729 canonization of John of Nepomuk, the patron saint of Bohemia. Benedict canonized an unusually large number as saints; Fontanini attributed eighteen to him.[1] This collection of texts was a summary rather

1. Fontanini includes the Venetian saint Lorenzo Giustiniani, who was canonized by Alexander VIII in 1690. See Patricia H. Labalme, "No Man but an Angel: Early Efforts to Canonize Lorenzo Giustiniani (1381–1456), in *Continuità e discontinuità nella storia, economica e religiosa: studi in onore di Aldo Stella* (Vicenza: Neri Pozza, 1993), 15–42, esp. 42.

than a critical analysis of the institutional role played by the papacy in the canonization of saints and the place of the saints in Catholic spirituality.

The whole issue of the status of saints, prophets, and holy men and women and of biography in general was a matter of interest to European readers. The publication of true histories, fiction and nonfiction, found a ready market in the book trade; in Catholic regions there was a lively interest in stories about saints and the miracles they had performed.[2] The patronage of the saints and of Mary had always been a concern in Catholic Europe; new special devotions to the Sacred Heart of Jesus and to the Holy Family responded to the increased importance of domesticity as a value in the patron-client relations of the eighteenth century. Reading lives of the saints was an important activity for the Catholic laity; more time was typically spent reading such works than Scripture. The significance of these holy figures in matters of local social solidarity made the celebration of their memory a contentious issue in church-state relations. A saint's feast was honored by religious celebrations and a holiday from work. Political entities, desirous of increasing revenues and of promoting a vibrant commerce, came to see these numerous celebrations aimed at enhancing an individual's spirituality as a drain on energies that could be devoted to enriching the general prosperity.

In the midst of so much printed matter about the lives of the good and the famous, clarity and standards were of particular importance to those charged with evaluating the narratives of the lives of religious figures who performed miracles while they were alive and after they were dead. In 1734, Cardinal Prospero Lambertini of Bologna published the first volume of his *De servorum dei beatificatione et beatorum canonizatione* (On the beatification of the servants of God and of the canonization of the blessed); the final volume, the fourth, appeared in 1738.[3] Lambertini had direct

2. Girolamo Imbruglia, "Dalle storie di santi alla storia naturale della religione: l'idea moderna di superstizione," *Rivista storica Italiana* 101 (1989), 35–84.

3. Mario Rosa, "Benedetto XIV," in *Dizionario biografico degli Italiani,* 8:393–408. See also Pietro Amato Frutaz, "Le principali edizioni e sinossi dei 'De servorum Dei beatificatione et de beatorum canonizatione': saggio per una bio-bibliografia critica," in *Benedetto XIV (Prospero Lambertini),* ed. Marco Cecchelli (Cento [Ferrara]: Centro Studi "Girolamo Baruffaldi," 1981), 1:27–90.

experience with the process of sanctification: he had held the office of Promoter of the Faith from 1708 to 1727, in which role he was responsible for evaluating proposed canonizations. He had been instrumental in putting together the case for Pope Pius V, who was canonized by Clement XII. No one doubted the former's piety, though his notorious lack of political prudence, exemplified by his excommunication of England's Queen Elizabeth I and then his claim to have also deposed and thus deprived her of the authority to govern, made his sainthood controversial. Lambertini also researched the dossier of Bologna's Catherine de'Vigri, or Catherine da Bologna, and worked for her canonization.[4] But he had blocked the sanctification of another Bolognese worthy, his fourteenth-century ancestor Imelda Lambertini. Given all his experience, it is not surprising that his opinion was sought on the Augustine matter. Fontanini printed the letter Lambertini wrote, dated August 23, 1727, supporting the claim that the body found in Pavia in 1695 was indeed that of Augustine.[5] This letter must have been instrumental when Benedict decided to proceed posthaste in the process of authenticating Augustine's relics. In 1727, Benedict XIII appointed Lambertini archbishop of Ancona and elevated him to be a cardinal in 1728. Subsequently he was elected pope in 1740; he selected the name Benedict XIV, in part to honor his patron. As pope he earned the respect of the European Republic of Letters; Voltaire dedicated his tragedy *Mahomet* to him, and Gibbon acknowledged his borrowings from Benedict's erudition.

De servorum dei began with a masterly bibliographical review of the scholarship of hagiography and a survey of writings about and collections of the lives of the saints. Lambertini first sought to define what was distinctive about Christian saintliness. He was emphatic that despite certain similarities, there was no historical or spiritual connection between the pagan ritual of apotheosis and its Christian or Catholic counterpart. He was aware of the attempt in certain Protestant circles and of libertines to reduce Catholicism to a variant of paganism: it was said that the cult of the saints was simply a deceit that made it possible for the ignorant to continue to believe in the old gods. To be sure, Lambertini rejected this view,

4. Serena Spanò Martinelli, "La canonizzazione di Caterina Vigri: un problema cittadino nella Bologna del seicento," in *Culto dei santi: istituzioni e classi sociali in età preindustriale*, ed. Sofia B. Gajano and Lucia Sebastiani (Roma: L. U. Japadre, 1984), 719–33.

5. Fulgenzio Bellelli, *Collectio actorum atque allegatorum . . .* , 2 vols. (Venice: Sebastiano Coleti, 1729), 347.

for he believed, among other things, that the Catholic faith was true and had brought to the world something quite distinct from pagan beliefs. He described the different kinds of holy men and women in the Christian tradition, the saints, martyrs, and confessors. Sanctification of these great individuals had at first been a local matter, he explained; but the sole power to certify sainthood shifted to Rome with Pope John XV's official canonization of Ulrich.

The issue of recognizing saintly virtue was scarcely controversial; celebrating noble, generous, and even unselfish actions of good people was easy to endorse. The claim, however, that miraculous cures and other supernatural signs were necessary manifestations of this virtue was an occasion of disagreement. Lambertini, relying on the latest works of medical science, sought to use this information as a positive aid in evaluating miracles. The truths of science, history, and the Catholic religion, he believed, could all be harmonized. He accepted the position implicit in the notorious Galileo ruling that all so-called natural laws of science, or for that matter the natural laws of human behavior proposed by many political theorists, must be understood as provisional and hypothetical because they were human interpretations of observations and behaviors. The claims of the likes of Spinoza that God could not change His own natural laws should not cow believers in revealed Scripture into accepting that the only alternative to Spinoza's views on natural law was to admit one's adherence to the irrational ignorance of the mob. To believe that some things in this world were beyond the understanding of natural philosophy was not tantamount to renouncing rationality. Lambertini sought to establish principles and a method by which human reason, properly guided, could identify true sanctity and distinguish remarkable and unusual natural occurrences from the genuinely miraculous.

Lambertini devoted a number of chapters to issues associated with the Translation of saints; the most recent he mentioned was the 1715 Translation of Pope Leo the Great to the Cappella della Colonna in St. Peter's. His detailed index contained several entries about Translation, but there were none for Invention, though he did discuss Inventions. The kind of narrative structure that had allowed Venice's patron saint, Mark, and the city-state's aristocratic regime to share the same public space and patriotic spirit was peripheral to Lambertini's concept of sainthood. What is clear from his method is that arguments relying on popular consent or on some form of the general will were not sufficient evidence in matters of sanctity, or for the judicial identification of relics. The cures and convulsions that occurred in 1728 at the Jansenist shrine at St. Médard in Paris might well be unusual, but they were not events beyond the power of nature.[6] Sainthood and the miracles of true saintliness were beyond the powers of nature; these signs could be recognized only by the testimony of an expert, whose assessment of the evidence was evaluated by other experts whose conclusions were reviewed by a bureaucratic process. The spontaneous acclamation of the people, the universal consensus of the community, while important for religious life, was not a distinct element in the formal or legal process that could confirm sainthood. More important than popular acclamation were the freedom of discussion and the admittance of different points of view during the process of evaluating evidence. But Lambertini also understood that sometimes decisions had to be made, and furthermore that prudence advised against any wholesale reevaluations of all traditions in the name of some abstract notion of the truth. His rigorous evaluation of evidence was different from the enthusiasm that had motivated Michele Colli to campaign on behalf of Augustine's relics. There is no evidence of Lambertini's opposition to the 1728 process followed in Pavia, but we know he believed that decisions on such matters should not be rushed.

A new opportunity to review what had transpired in Pavia arrived serendipitously in 1743, when scholars writing the *Acta sanctorum* completed the volumes for the end of August, which included the feast day of St. Augustine. The *Acta sanctorum* is the major work written by the Bollandist Fathers, who still operate the longest-lived European institute of advanced research. The idea for this project of collecting, critically editing, and publishing the texts of the lives of all the saints was formulated in the early seventeenth century. The fundamental decisions about how to realize this research project were laid out by John Bolland. After a variety of ways of organizing this material were considered, it was decided to arrange the lives of the saints by the calendar; the life of each saint could be found in the volume, which listed the saint's feast day. There was a practical kind of rationale to this system, but it soon became clear that it posed unusual

6. Robert Kreiser, *Miracles, Convulsions and Ecclesiatical Politics in Early Eighteenth-Century France* (Princeton: Princeton University Press, 1978); and Catherine-Laurence Maire, ed., *Les convulsionnaires de Saint-Médard: miracles, convulsions et prophéties à Paris au XVIIe siècle* (Paris: Gallimard, 1985).

challenges to the researcher. To edit the texts about a life properly, the researcher would have to master the languages, dialects, geography, chronology, history, and culture of a specific region. The next "life" that that researcher prepared would, more than likely, require mastering an entirely different expertise. The variety of the subject matter must have been exhilarating for the working groups of scholars who would cooperatively produce the lives and edit the texts. Bolland's pupil Godefroid Henskens, or Henschenius, joined him; they were both Jesuits from the Flanders area. All the subsequent Bollandists, taking their name from their founder, were of the same religious order and from the same region. The first three volumes of the *Acta*, covering the entire month of January, were published in 1643; the February volumes followed in 1658. The numbers of volumes required to encompass subsequent months increased: August was in six volumes. A reprint of all the completed volumes was printed in Venice; another updated reprint followed in the mid-nineteenth century.

The Bollandists published their volume containing St. Augustine in 1743. The narrative of his life had been begun by Guilielmus Cuperus (Kuyper); he had reached chapter 37 when he suddenly died. The remainder was completed by Johanes Stiltingo (Jean Stiltingh), who became the leader of the Bollandists in the middle years of the eighteenth century. The article on Augustine runs some 250 folio pages. It is in sixty-five chapters and includes the biography written by Possidius and some thirty-five folio pages of excerpts from the *Confessions*. The Bollandist life spent chapters reviewing the scholarly and theological controversies that had developed from subsequent interpretations of Augustine's actions and writings. The article began with a review of the publishing history of the saint's biographies. The Bollandists did not challenge Augustine's statements about his lack of Greek, but they did itemize those instances when he showed knowledge of that language. The article proceeded more or less chronologically through the major events of his life. If specific books were subsequently the occasion for theological controversy, that history was traced and, when appropriate, it was noted how the dispute was concluded, often with reference to a definitive papal decision.

After describing Augustine's conversion, baptism, his sabbatical at Cassiciacum, and his subsequent return to Thagaste in Africa, the authors devoted chapters 14 through 16 to the quarrel between the Augustinian Hermits and the Canons Regular. The different versions of the foundations of both orders were described; and it was noted that what one order affirmed, the other denied, and vice versa. Recalcitrance and reprehensible behavior characterized both sides, the Bollandists charged, explaining that the weakness in the evidence for both cases made it imprudent to essay a judgment as to which side, if either, had the better case. At this time, lives of Augustine would often discuss his dual Translation; the *Acta* devoted three chapters to these events and to the placement of the body in San Pietro. The various texts about the body's being hidden were also reviewed. Chapters 60 and 61 discussed the 1695 Invention, the subsequent controversy, and Benedict XIII's role in resolving the matter in 1728, but no mention was made of Muratori's intervention.[7] The chapter following the discussion of the Invention controversy concerned the miracles associated with the 1695 Invention. The locations of other relics of St. Augustine were mentioned, and still another chapter included texts about other apparitions and miracles attributed to St. Augustine. The article ended with a bibliography of Augustine's writings.

One of the strengths of the Bollandists and a genuine contribution to the discourse of ecclesiastical history was their recognition that debate and disagreement were often a sign of strength, not of failure or betrayal, in matters of the history of religion. And they understood that the resolute defense of an opinion supported by evidence might well conflict with another interpretation also having serious justifications. There was no reason, they believed, to blush with embarrassment, to forge the lacking evidence, or to retreat into silence because there could be no agreement on the right answer; there was no need to despair and embrace skepticism because human reason could not provide definitive guidance on what we believe we need to know about religion. The absence of a conclusion did not mean that there was an absolute limit to our understanding of the matter. Instead, the proper conclusion was a provisional statement recognizing that what was known or done at one time might change, but that change need not invalidate what had been handled differently before. This openness did not extend to other religious traditions, however. For them, the true religion might well have a significant history, but other faiths and religious traditions did not possess history in this sense; theirs was but a chronicle of error and deceit.

7. These chapters have now been translated. Joannes Stiltingh, "The Account in the 'Acta sanctorum' of the Body of St. Augustine," trans. Joseph C. Schnaubelt and Frederick Van Fleteren, in *Augustine in Iconography: History and Legend,* ed. Joseph C. Schnaubelt and Frederick Van Fleteren (New York: Peter Lang, 1999), 65–112.

By no stretch of the imagination was the *Acta sanctorum* a popular work or one that was readily accessible to the general reader. But the documents selected for inclusion do contain testimonies of non-clerics and include examples of what we would call popular culture. The Bollandists compiled both the popular and the learned recollections of near contemporaries concerning the holy men and women of the past as well as the views, evaluations, and critiques of trained experts. Much of the material they presented was textual, but they would also reproduce and interpret manuscript illustrations and other images. Of course, they had practically no access to direct verbal testimony, but in their collection of extracts there was a clear commitment to presenting a broad selection of the variety of evidence that had been uncovered. Their presentation of many kinds of narratives and their willingness to record a variety of experiences were typical of the impartiality and openness of their work. The Bollandists made a serious effort to record popular traditions, and they did not hesitate to criticize those practices that seemed without firm Christian foundations. They preserved these records with the aim of finding the truth, whether the evidence came from a member of the elite or from the people. Their work thus preserved popular beliefs and traditional practices, even though they had no special interest in such sources or in recreating what we would call the mentalities of peasants or the urban poor.

Catholic biographers continued to be drawn to the task of explaining the meaning of Augustine's life. Most of the authors were Augustinian Hermits trying to set the record straight. The Augustinian Lorenzo Berti published his *De rebus gestis S. Augustini latinorum patrum nobilissimi librisque ab eodem conscriptis commentarius* in Venice in 1756.[8] The publisher was Antonio Bassanese. Berti began by reviewing all the major lives of Augustine that had been published. Among his purposes was to correct the bad or at least slovenly impression a reader might gain from reading Le Clerc's essay on the Maurist edition of his work. Not only did Augustine know Greek, he argued, but also he had a competency in Hebrew. And Augustine was not a drunk, though Berti admitted he might have, on occasion, been tempted to eat too much. Typical of his approach was

8. R. P. B. van Luijk, "Gianlorenzo Berti, agostiniano (1696–1766)," *Rivista di storia della chiesa in Italia* 14 (1960), 235–62, 383–410.

his evaluation of the delightful story about the composition of the famous hymn the *Te Deum:* according to tradition, both Ambrose and Augustine sang it as an *ex tempore* duet when Ambrose lifted Augustine above the baptismal waters. Some, he noted, had denied that the work was written on that occasion, and others doubted the saints' reputed authorship. Still, Berti continued, the whole story may not have been apocryphal; there may have been, and probably was, some truth to it. He cited respected authorities who agreed with the traditional account.

But his real point in writing this work was not to answer a variety of minor objections about Augustine's life. In this work of seventy-six chapters, twenty-five of them deal with Augustine's role as the founder of the Augustinian Hermits, which Berti believed occurred in 390. Thus he implicitly denied the claim of the Canons Regular to being the first Augustinian order. Berti was a thoughtful reader of Augustine's works, and not surprisingly, he saw the author of *The Confessions* as primarily a legislator for his religious community. He was an abbot first and a bishop second. Augustine, he wrote, was an exemplary individual, perfect in his kind, an ideal type; for Berti, Augustine was not yet the precursor of the romantic notion of individuality and of self-disclosure. In this Berti is closer in spirit to the traditional artistic representations of Augustine in which he wears the regalia of a bishop.

In 1767, in Madrid, Francisco Antonio de Gante, an Augustinian Hermit, published his own biography of Augustine: *El monstruo de Africa indefinibile: vica de S. Augustin obispo, y doctor de la Iglesia, funda de la orden de los Ermitanos Augustinos* (The indefinable African prodigy: the life of St. Augustine, bishop, doctor of the church, and founder of the Augustinian Hermits). As with Berti, of central importance to him was to prove the temporal priority of the Augustinian Hermits over the Canons, and to prove that the Hermits were the ones most truly loved by Augustine. The last pages of the work (407–35) concern Augustine's Translations and the Invention. De Gante presents the familiar story favoring the dates of Baronius. He links Augustine with the Hebrew patriarch Joseph, whose name, he explains, comes from a Hebrew word meaning "increase," just as the name Augustine also derived from the Greek verb "to increase."

The Benedictines of St. Maur produced their own very influential collection of lives of the saints in the middle of the eighteenth century. This was the *Histoire générale des auteurs sacrés et ecclésiastiques;* the ninth volume was devoted to St. Augustine. No mention is made of Augustine as a founder of either the Hermits or the Canons Regular, though the author mentions the monastic communities he did establish. The only reference to the Translation and Invention of his body occurs in footnotes added by subsequent editors of this work in the nineteenth century. In a volume of almost nine hundred pages, only twenty are allotted to the story of his life; most of the rest is a summary of his writings. A decade later a creative rethinking of the autobiographical genre appeared with the publication of Rousseau's *Confessions*. Rousseau, in his paradoxical fashion, borrowed another man's title for a work he claimed to be unique and forever inimitable. Rousseau, in some of his books, articulated a theory of political life and social organization based on a love between people which integrates thoughts Augustine expressed in *The City of God*. After Rousseau, Augustine's *Confessions* would never be the same book again. Augustine's bones were also buffeted and tossed about by other new winds coming out of France.

In 1733, Pavia was caught up in the helter-skelter of the War of the Polish Succession, which altered the political fortunes of southern Italy and of Parma and Piacenza. An army of French soldiers and troops of the kingdom of Sardinia (this political entity, with its capital at Turin, was also referred to as both Savoy and Piedmont) occupied Lombardy. For a brief period San Pietro was used as a hospital by the French, and St. Augustine was moved in February 1734 to the Duomo for safekeeping. On August 30, 1734, the bones were returned to San Pietro. After the war was over and the Austrians were returned to power in Lombardy, work was resumed on the new altar, which was finished in 1738. Political boundaries were redrawn, and Piedmont (or Sardinian territory) came all the way to the Ticino River. Pavia, now a border town, continued its position as one of the sites, though not an important one, of the traditional pilgrimage route for French Catholics crossing northern Italy.[9] The new Sardinian lands on the other side of the Ticino remained under the spiritual authority of the bishop of Pavia and continued for some time to receive priests who were

9. Dominique Julia, "Pour une géographie européenne du pèlerinage à l'époque moderne et contemporaine," in *Pèlerins et pèlerinages dans l'Europe moderne: actes de la table ronde organisée par le Départment d'histoire et civilisation de l'Institut universitaire européen de Florence et l'École française de Rome (Rome, 4–5 juin 1993)* (Rome: École française de Rome, 2000), 1–126, esp. 107 and 125 on Pavia.

trained at the seminary of the diocese of Pavia. Later, Sardinia's rulers decided not to continue to accept priests from an Austrian-dominated region, and so they created their own seminary at Valenza in 1787. In this way they could avoid the "Austrian" priests, as they called those who were trained in Pavia. Giuseppe Bertieri, appointed bishop of Pavia in 1792, was a rigid Augustinian and, some hoped, a Jansenist. His fairness disappointed the radicals.[10] Since Pavia's seminary had been closed, he opened a new one at San Pietro for his entire diocese, but it was shut down by Napoleon at the end of the century. In 1801, Bertieri participated in the reorganization of the Cisalpine Republic, the regime created by the French to govern northern Italy. Bertieri sought to work with the variety of political entities that ruled there, but his efforts to provide trained clergy for his parishes were overwhelmed by the general decline in religious vocations. The number of clergy in the diocese of Pavia dropped: in 1782, the numbers had been 67.5 clergy per 10,000 people; in 1823 the figure had declined to 37 per 10,000.[11]

Other influences from outside Italy were to have a direct impact on the communities of San Pietro and the relics of Augustine. In the 1780s, Pavia became the center for the reform attempted by the emperor of Austria, Joseph II, concerning church-state relations.[12] Among his aims was to bring about an institutional reform of religious life and to preserve only those religious orders that were truly useful to the state. One instrument he developed for this purpose was the appointment of certain theologians and academics to the faculty at the University of Pavia. He expected the university to produce a new generation of public administrators who would hold the same values as their teachers. It might seem surprising that Joseph turned to Jansenism, a movement identified with a personal, confessional

10. Giuseppe Pignatelli, "Bertieri, Giuseppe," in *Dizionario biografico degli italiani,* 9:526–28.

11. Xenia Toscani, *Aspetti di vita religiosa a Pavia nel secolo XV* (Milan: A. Giuffrè, 1969), 306–6, 329.

12. Marco Bernuzzi, *La facoltà teologica dell'università di Pavia nel periodo delle riforme (1767–1797)* (Milan: Istituto Editoriale Cisalpino–La Goliardica, 1983). Ettore Rotta, "Il Giansenismo dell'Università pavese e la questione religiose nella repubblica cisalpina," *Bolletino della Società pavese di storia patria* 6 (1906), 564–608. On the impact of this reform on another region in Lombardy, Lodi, see Lucia Sebastiani, "Culto dei santi, feste religiose e comunità nella Lombardia," in Gajano and Sebastiani, *Culto dei santi,* 789–833. On Joseph's program for the monasteries north of the Alps, see Derek Beales, "Joseph II and the Monasteries of Austria and Hungary," in *Religious Change in Europe, 1650–1914,* ed. Nigel Aston (Oxford: Clarendon Press, 1997), 161–84.

approach to religious expression, to spearhead a reform of the public administration and of the temporal activities and powers of religious orders. A modern reader may be even more amazed that Joseph could imagine that the faculty of a university could play a direct, practical role in bringing about a transformation of church-state relations. It should be kept in mind that few models existed for the kind of project Joseph sought to implement, and given the presuppositions of most enlightened reformers, the expectation that a professor of theology or of philosophy might serve as the bellwether for a more rational form of state administration would not have appeared as naïve as it might to us.[13]

The intellectual group that supported Joseph's project was a rather different movement from that of the French Jansenists of the previous century.[14] The Italian Jansenists lacked the volatile mood swings of their French predecessors, who would carom from morbid depression to wild excitability in response to too much concentration on humanity's unworthiness of salvation. The Italian emphasis was on the desirability of rigid moral principles, the value of labor, and the belief that true religious spirituality was best promoted by a clear separation of church and state in which the church recognized the authority of the state in all political matters. This political Jansenism, like the original movement, was primarily the concern of an educated elite. They never made any headway in altering Catholic orthodoxy, but these Jansenists proved extremely successful in legal quarrels, dominating important committees and appeals panels in Rome. In the early eighteenth century, they succeeded in undermining the Jesuit plan to train Chinese priests in a seminary in which the teaching would be conducted in the Chinese language. Under Jansenist influence it was decided that the only proper language for the training of a priest was Latin and that the education of Chinese priests should take place near Rome. Therefore a college for Chinese priests was established in Naples in 1732. Special rites in native languages for the promulgation of Catholicism in the sophisticated civilizations of East Asia were replaced by the Latin Rite; in 1715 and 1742 edicts removed non-Latin rites practiced in China, and in 1744 their use in India was sharply curtailed. The

13. An interesting view of the reform movement is Carlo Pilati's proposal to transform northern Italy. See Franco Venturi, *Settecento riformatore,* vol. 2, *La chiesa e la repubblica dentro i loro limiti* (Turin: Einaudi, 1976), 2:274–325.

14. Arturo Carlo Jemolo, *Il Giansenismo in Italia prima della rivoluzione* (Bari: Laterza, 1928).

laity, however, rejected pastoral Jansenism, finding its principles incompatible with most popular religious practice.

Both Joseph II and the Jansenists brought a moralistic impulse to their reform. Seventeenth-century French Jansenism had had strong connections with political interests that emphasized local or at least an antiroyalist bias. Joseph, by contrast, did not dither over the sensitivities and sensibilities of local authorities or traditional rights and privileges of provinces and other local political entities; the enlightened administrator, the agents of the monarch, had the undisputed right to implement change. The challenge facing all Catholic religious orders from such reformers was already clear in Rome's 1773 dissolution of the Jesuit order. To be sure, the papacy had submitted to this only under extreme diplomatic compulsion, and was secretly quite pleased that Russia and Prussia had given refuge to members of that order. The Jansenist faction was delighted with this turn of events and used it to further their campaign to dispossess other religious orders and members of the clergy of property and other wealth that served no clear godly function. They also sought to compel monastic orders to adhere to their vows, to close individual monasteries whose membership had declined, and to consolidate them with others of the same order. Rome had yielded to this pressure and had gradually reduced the number of fast days and holy days, besides Sunday, on which work was forbidden. In 1783, Pius VI abolished some thirty holy days and set the number of obligatory feast days (non-workdays) other than Sundays at nineteen. On other feast days Catholics might be required to attend the Mass, but they would also be permitted to work.

Joseph II had far-reaching plans for implementing his vision of how a reformed Catholic Church could be harmonized with his conception of the rationally administered state. Reform of the state bureaucracy and the judicial system was essential to the completion of his project. Joseph turned to the University of Pavia to create the centers for the energy and new ideas needed to realize this ambition.[15] Martino Natali, a priest who taught

15. Since 1778, one of Italy's most prestigious scientists, Alessandro Volta, had been on the faculty. Giambattista Biffi was one of Pavia's outstanding graduates whose thoughtful and alert observations remain useful in understanding the turbulent decades of the 1760s and 1770s. See Franco Venturi, *Settecento riformatore,* vol. 5, *L'italia dei lumi (1764–1790),* pt. 1, *La rivoluzione di Corsica: le grande carestie degli anni sessanta: la Lombardia delle riforme* (Turin: Einaudi, 1987), 725–40 (on Volta), 667–84 (on Biffi). The Scottish traveler Joseph Forsyth identified Pavia as "the present metropolis of Italian science"; see *Remarks on An-*

moral theology, Giuseppe Zola, who taught ecclesiastical history, and Pietro Tamburini, who chaired the theology faculty, were all appointed to the faculty of the University of Pavia in the 1780s.[16] They were all so-called Jansenists, and, to look at their careers, it seems that if one wanted to obtain tenure at the University of Pavia it was necessary to have a book on Rome's Index of Condemned Books. Zola and Tamburini came from Brescia in Venetian territory, and, in their view, Lombardy offered more intellectual freedom than was available in the more conservative Republic of Venice.

As part of Joseph's plan to consolidate monastic houses, in 1785 the Canons Regular were removed from Pavia. For the first time the Augustinian Hermits had Augustine to themselves. But in October 1786, the Hermits were ordered to occupy the former house of the Jesuits, which had become vacant when their order was suppressed. The Augustinians took the relics of Augustine and Boethius and the *arca* with them. Their possession of Augustine was no longer a joint responsibility. The absence of the Canons gave them no holiday, though Joseph had no interest in quarreling over Augustine. Centuries of institutionalized disagreement had ended. The Hermits had the bones, and as for Pavia, Augustine remained its patron. His relics were still regarded as desirable and a matter of status: a piece of Augustine's right foot was given by Pavia's Bishop Bartolomeo Olivazzi to the duke of Parma in 1789. An order of Dominicans was lodged in San Pietro; they stayed for a couple of years before being moved elsewhere. Even at the point when the saint's church was taken from him, there are indications that Augustine's memory was still

---

tiquities, Arts, and Letters during an Excursion in Italy in the Years 1802 and 1803 by Joseph Forsyth, Esq., ed. Keith Crook (Newark: University of Delaware Press, 2001), 241. The emperor's project for creating this seat of learning and reforming the university went back to the 1740s. See Alessandro Visconti, "L'opera del governo austriaco nella riforma universitaria durante il ventennio 1753–1773," in *Contributi alla storia dell'Università di Pavia: pubblicati nell'XI centenario dell'Ateneo* (Pavia: Tipografia Cooperativa, 1925), 175–238; for the final phases, 230–38.

16. Paolo Guerrini, "Carteggi Bresciani inediti sulla vita e i tempi di Pietro Tamburini (1737–1827)," *Bolletino della Società pavese di storia patria* 27 (1927), 161–250. Ettore Rotta, "Per la riforma degli studi eclesiastici nell'Università pavese al tempo di Giuseppe II," *Bollettino della Società pavese di storia patria* 7 (1907), 402–12. Ettore Rotta, "Pietro Tamburini di Brescia 'teologo piacentino' e la controversia Giansenista a Piacenza," *Bolletino della Società pavese di storia patria* 12 (1912), 343–64. Jemolo, *Il Giansenismo in Italia prima della rivoluzione,* esp. chap. 6, 263–347.

celebrated in Pavia. On St. Augustine's feast date, August 28, 1789, at the Nuovo Teatro, there was a performance of *Una cosa rara ossia Bellezza ed onestà* (A Rare Thing: Beauty and Virtue in the Same Person), with music by Vincenzo Martin y Soler; the libretto was published in Pavia by Pietro Galeazzi.[17] The advertisement and program for the production made no explicit reference to Augustine. Late August was not the opera season, but in Pavia at least, the saint's day required a festive display. Augustine's feast day had become part of the rhythm of life in Pavia. It was as if the quarrels between the two orders and the more recent debate over the identity of the bones had not obscured the meaning of St. Augustine for Pavia. Augustine was not just a particular cache of bones; his presence was felt by Pavians. Modern studies in the history of religion have taught us that responses of this kind are part of what we understand to be an aspect of the phenomenon of religion. It is recognized that music and poetry have been used as metaphors for and ways to provide access to, and commemorate the meaning contained in, myth and religious experience. For about a century, off and on, Pavia seemed compelled as if by some cultural pattern to celebrate spontaneously the memory of its patron Augustine on his feast day.

San Pietro had no religious order attached to it as permanent residents. For a time in the 1790s, part of its buildings served as the diocesan seminary. There is some evidence that Franciscans (*minori conventuali*) occupied part of San Pietro in the 1790s as well. Then in the early summer of 1796 farmers took over Pavia, making clear their opposition to the reforms and the regime of the French and their supporters. On May 23, as part of the tumult of the insurrection, an Augustinian Hermit was said to have killed four French soldiers.[18] On May 1, 1799, Napoleon expelled the Hermits from Pavia. The relics of Augustine were moved to the Duomo under the care of Bishop Bertieri, who was also an Augustinian Hermit. (In

17. Guido Bustico, "I teatri musicali di Pavia," *Bollettino della Società pavese di storia patria* 3 (1903), 81–102, esp. 96. *Cosa rara* is known today primarily because a tune from this opera is played by the onstage orchestra in the last scene of Mozart's *Don Giovanni.*

18. Giancarlo Marinoni, "La situazioni patrimoniale delle comunità religiose in territorio pavese alla fine del secolo XVIII," *Bollettino della Società pavese di storia patria,* n.s. 5 (1953), 80–99, esp. 85–86. Faustino Gianini, "Un diario del 'Sacco del 1796,'" *Bollettino della Società pavese di storia patria* 28 (1928), 337–49, esp. 343.

October of that year, at the time Augustine's Translation was usually celebrated, an opera buffa was performed called *Il furbo contro il furbo*, "Theft against Theft.") Some of the art in San Pietro's was sold; today, certain of these items can be seen in Milanese museums. The sculpted *arca*, too, was almost broken up and sold; instead it was crated and put in storage, all but forgotten. Napoleon, in a decree of 3 Thermidor, Year 9 (1803), made public his plan to turn the complex of buildings at San Pietro into a military school. The cloister of the Hermits was destroyed, while that of the Canons Regular became the central building of this new military school.[19] The church was used to store fodder, munitions, and other supplies.

Even without the presence of the rival religious orders, new controversies over the ownership of Augustine's bones arose. Siro Comi, the archivist of Pavia, an acknowledged master of Italian literary history, a translator of Rousseau, and a supporter of the new French-backed regime, took the issue of the bones in a new direction.[20] In 1803 he published in Pavia *Memoria storico-diplomatica, letta e presentata da Siro Comi al Municipale suo consesso sul diritto del Pubblico di Pavia al deposito e all'Arca del gran Vescovo d'Ippona, Sant'Agostino* (A historical and documentary monograph read and presented by Siro Comi to the city concerning its consent on the right of the citizens of Pavia to the remains and *arca* of the famous bishop of Hippo, St. Augustine). His argument was that the people of Pavia, the *commune*, were and always had been the real proprietors of Augustine's bones and of the *arca*. All the Translations of the body from Liutprand down to Napoleon had been carried out with the consent and witness of the people, who authorized these various moves through the municipal government. He wanted to make clear that while the bones and the *arca* were now housed in the Duomo, the bishop had no claim or right to these sacred treasures; he simply held them in trust for the citizens. The various changes of the religious orders residing in San Pietro had also been made with the approval of the people: that was the significance of the people's presence at the processions that marked the various Translations of the

19. Giovanni Mantese, "Rivoluzione francese e crisi del Giansenismo italiano da un carteggio inedito di Francesco Alpruni, professore all'università di Pavia," *Bolletino storico pavese* 5 (1942), 41–64.

20. Pietro Cabrini, "Comi, Siro," in *Dizionario biografico degli Italiani,* 27:565–67. See also Maria de Bernardi, "Un secolo di erudizione pavese, 1750–1850," *Bolletino della Società pavese di storia patria,* n.s. 1 (1936), 35–72. Siro Comi, *Del pubblico di Pavia al deposito e all'Arca del gran Vescovo d'Ippona Sant'Agostino* (Pavia: Bolzani, 1803).

relics. And, furthermore, the *arca* was public property, not the possession of the Hermits or their successors.

Comi was promptly answered by an ecclesiastic who published that same year in Milan his *Notizie sincere e documentale sul traporto alla cattedrale di Pavia, del Sacro Deposito, altare ed Arca di Sant'Agostino, con alcune osservazioni sul libro intitolato: "Memoria storico-diplomatica letta e presentata da Siro Comi"* (An honest account supported by documents of the conveyance to the Cathedral of Pavia the sacred remains, altar, and *arca* of St. Augustine, with some observations on the book "The historical and documentary monograph read and presented by Siro Comi"). The author strongly disputed Comi's analysis of the facts. He refuted Comi's claim that the key given to the officials of the *comune* by Benedict XIII had conferred the ongoing ownership of the relics and sculptures to the city. Comi, he said, had twisted the obvious meaning of the document. The pope had established in 1728 that the bones being cared for in San Pietro were those of St. Augustine, and Pertusati, the bishop of Pavia, had given the key not to bestow a right on the city but to recognize its concern for one of the city's patron saints. In 1804, Comi published a refutation, *Il diritto e possesso del pubblico di Pavia sul deposito e sull'Arca di Sant'Agostino, vescovo d'Ippone, difese e confermati da Siro Comi contro le opposizioni proposte da un Capitulare della Cattedrale nel libro intitolato: "Notizie sincere e documentate"* (The right and possession by the people of Pavia of the relics and the *arca* of St. Augustine, bishop of Hippo, defended and confirmed by Siro Comi against the opposition by a member of the Cathedral Chapter House titled "An honest account supported by documents"). Comi restated his position and printed the documents, which he believed spoke for themselves, to show the obvious correctness of his interpretation.

After the fall of Napoleon and the end of French occupation, the Austrians returned to Lombardy; some of the remaining buildings of San Pietro were restored to clerical use. In 1822 a performance of *Il turco in Italia* was held on St. Augustine's feast day, although nothing explicitly linked the performance to the saint.[21] In 1825 the old chapter house of the Canons Regular became, once again, the seminary for training priests for the diocese of Pavia.[22] Defendente Sacchi and his cousin Giuseppe wrote

21. Bustico, "I teatri musicali di Pavia," 3, 208–33, esp. 220.

22. Faustino Gianani, *La basilica di S. Pietro in Ciel d'Oro di Pavia nella storia e nell'arte* (Pavia: Fusi, 1983), 6.

a work on architecture, *Saggio intorno all'architectura* (An essay on architecture) with an emphasis on the contribution of the Lombards; it was published in Milan in 1828. This book was followed by the first modern study of the *arca, L'arca storiche di Pavia* (The renowned *arca* of Pavia); it was published in Pavia in 1832.[23] This latter volume was written on the occasion of the placement of the *arca* and of Augustine's relics in their own chapel in the Duomo, which has since been destroyed. The *arca* was described as a work of art and as part of the broader patterns of the artistic production and styles of fourteenth-century Lombard sculpture. It was not discussed as an ideological representation of the history of the Hermits and of their right to the undisputed control of Augustine's relics. Throughout the 1830s, San Pietro seemed on the verge of being demolished for its brick and other building materials. These threats were finally averted when the construction workers themselves refused to destroy the work of their ancestors. The memory of the divided cultural space of San Pietro had been replaced by the conception of the building as a monument, a treasure of the city's past that deserved preservation. In 1842, Bishop Luigi Tosi presented the right ulna of Augustine to the new bishop of Hippo, Augustine's successor, Antonio Adolfo Dupuch, who was appointed to open a new church in what was now the French colony of Algeria.

In 1859, on the occasion of the war between Austria, Piedmont (Savoy), and France over Austria's role in northern Italy, the buildings of San Pietro once again reverted to military uses. The seminary, the Canons' old chapter house, again became a military hospital, and San Pietro was once again used as a military magazine. After the war the church was used to store straw and forage. Cesare Prelini wrote a new work on the *arca* in 1871, *Le ceneri e l'arca di San Agostino* (The ashes and *arca* of St. Augustine); this was followed by his study of San Pietro in 1877, *L'insigne basilica e monastero di S. Pietro in Ciel d'Oro* (The imposing basilica and monastery of San Pietro in Ciel d'Oro). Then, on December 4, 1877, part of the vault of San Pietro collapsed, threatening the façade; the right nave had been in a state

23. On Defendente Sacchi, see de Bernardi, "Un secolo di erudizione pavese," 57–86, esp. 73. A second edition of the Sacchis' work on the *arca* appeared in 1833. Earlier in the 1820s, Defendente Sacchi published in Pavia the *Collezione dei classici metafisici;* his brother translated three works of Destutt de Tracy, a French liberal and philosophe who inspired a new generation of Italian revolutionaries. Both men played an influential role as journalists in Milan in the 1820s and 1830s.

of progressive collapse for most of the century. A citizen's group had been organized to raise money to save San Pietro and in June 1884 restoration work was begun. Also in 1884, Crisanto Zuradelli published a history of the Basilica of San Pietro.[24] The aim of the restoration was to return the church, as much as possible, to its twelfth-century design; hence the floor was restored to its original level, and the Romanesque interior was restored, as were the many delightful capitals carved with the images of beasts.[25] This restoration is what we see in San Pietro today.

Cardinal Agostino Gaetano Riboldi held one final *recognizione canonica* (an investigation in accordance with canon law) of Augustine's relics in 1884. A Professor Mazzucchelli, who taught anatomy at the university, assisted him. Two hundred and twenty-five pieces of bone were counted; remarkably, some of the glass vials still emitted a pleasing odor.[26] By the nineteenth century, opera, which had been primarily performed in Carnival time in the eighteenth century, had acquired a regular fall and Lenten season in Pavia. Operas were also sometimes performed in the August holidays. Although no special mention of Augustine was made on the program, on St. Augustine's feast day, August 28, 1880, Verdi's *Attila* was staged in a special performance at the Fraschini Theater.[27] On June 15, 1896, San Pietro was reopened and Cardinal Riboldi, bishop of Pavia, celebrated the Mass. The crypt altar area had been reconstructed so that it could support the weight of the *arca,* which was to be placed on the main altar. On October 7, 1900, one traditional date of Liutprand's Translation of the bones, the relics of St. Augustine were translated once again from the Duomo back to San Pietro in Ciel d'Oro.[28] This time the bones of Augustine, the

24. Crisanto Zuradelli, *La basilica di S. Pietro in Ciel d'Oro ed i suoi ricordi storici* (Pavia: Fratelli Fusi, 1884).

25. Gianani, *La basilica di S. Pietro,* 78–79.

26. Riboldi wrote his own account of the major relics in Pavia. See Agostino Riboldi, *I tre venerabili sepolcri di S. Siro, S. Agostino e S. Severino Boezio nella cattedrale di Pavia* (Pavia, 1885).

27. Bustico, "I teatri musicali di Pavia," 5 (1905), 43–80, esp. 70. *Attila* is the only grand opera to have a part for a Father of the Church: Pope Leo the Great, a bass, appears and persuades Attila to spare Rome. In the first performances censors demanded that Leo be presented simply as an old man, not as a pope. I do not know what performance practices were followed in this production.

28. *Le feste celebrate in Pavia per le solenne traslaz. delle Rel. di S. Agostino dalla Cattedrale* (Rome: Vaticana, 1900).

relics of Boethius, and the *arca* were entrusted to Alfonso Semenza, the prior of an order of Augustinian Hermits who took up residence with his monks at San Pietro. Since that time the Augustinian Hermits have been the sole order residing there. Ritual was thus restored to San Pietro, though it is the Hermits alone who offer the ongoing care of St. Augustine's bones. The Hermits have built a fine library devoted to the history of their order and its vibrant spiritual mission. No attempt was made to revive John XXII's unconventional experiment in institutional strife.

Quarrels related to St. Augustine's relics reappeared in a modified form in the late nineteenth and early twentieth centuries. The papacy had not welcomed the new Italian state, at least in the form in which it developed. In 1868 the papacy forbade Catholics to participate actively in the political life of the new Italian nation; at least that was one interpretation. Not surprisingly, this conflict of church and state prompted scholars to research its historical origins. The bitter struggles between the Guelphs and the Ghibellines, the papacy and the emperor, became a subject of especial historical study, and Dante, a Ghibelline, became enshrined as the first poet of a united Italy in the educational curriculum of state-sponsored schools.[29] The Guelph-Ghibelline quarrel inspired reinterpretations of Pavian history as well. Giacinto Romano, who was soon to be appointed to the history faculty of the University of Pavia, in an 1895 article on the quarrel between the Canons and the Hermits in the fourteenth century, presented the splitting of San Pietro as part of the contest between the papacy and the empire. And his interpretation of the war between the Visconti and Monferrato portrayed the Hermits as supporters of local interests, with the Canons supporting the Visconti and Milan the empire.[30] Present-day interpreters of these events place less emphasis on the political allegiances of these orders and describe both the Canons and the Hermits as victims of the militaristic policies of the German emperor.

29. Ilaria Porciani, "Il medioevo nella costruzione dell'Italia unita: la proposta di un mito," in *Italia e Germania: immagini, modelli, miti fra due popoli nell'ottocento: il Medioevo; Das Mittelalter: Ansichten, Stereotypen und Mythen zweier Völker im neunzehnten Jahrhundert: Deutschland und Italien,* ed. Reinhard Elze and Pierangelo Schiera (Bologna: Il Mulino, 1988), 163–91.

30. Giacinto Romano, "Eremitani e canonici regolari in Pavia nel secolo XIV e loro attinenze con la loro cittadina," *Archivio storico lombardo* ser. 3, vol. 4, year 22 (1895), 5–42.

In 1901, three months after the restoration of St. Augustine's bones in San Pietro, the Società pavese di Storia Patria (the Pavian local history society) was founded. Its membership list included mostly men of the professional elite; some were members of the clergy, though none were Hermits. The bylaws stated that there were to be annual meetings, and the society's primary printed communication to the learned was to be a scholarly journal. There were 180 individual members as well as two associations included in the membership list. This probably did not include all the likely readers of the journal; the size of the audience for the journal was probably not very different from the numbers who read religiously about the original controversy over St. Augustine's bones. Giacinto Romano, now a professor at the University of Pavia, was the first president; the secretary was Rodolfo Maiocchi, conservator of the Civic Museum, who later joined the history faculty at Pavia; and the vice secretary was Ferruccio Quintavalle, a teacher at the *liceo.* Romano had been born in Eboli near Salerno in 1854; he first taught at the *liceo* in Pavia before being called to the University of Messina. In 1900 he was invited to join the history faculty at the University of Pavia. The primary responsibility of the secretary was the publication of the society's journal, the *Bollettino.* Maiocchi was a native of Pavia, born in 1862; among his ancestors were a number of illustrious historians and local antiquarians. Both Romano and Maiocchi cooperated in creating the new Società, and they led a major project to publish the primary documents pertinent to the history of the University of Pavia, *Codice diplomatica dell'università di Pavia* (The manuscript statutes of the University of Pavia).

The first article in the society's *Bollettino* was a piece by Romano on why Pavia became the capital of the Lombard kings. Also in this issue was an article by the university librarian, Luigi de Marchi, concerning a manuscript important in the Augustine controversy, known as the *Anonimo ticinese* or *Anonymi ticinensis, liber de laudibus civitatis ticenensis* (The anonymous Pavian, "A book in celebration of Pavia").[31] It had originally been published in the eleventh volume of Muratori's *Rerum italicarum scriptores,* published in 1727; the text had been edited by Beretti, based on a copy prepared by the notary Michelangelo Canevari as part of research done in 1698 in the first attempt to determine the authenticity of Augus-

31. Luigi de Marchi, "I manoscritti dell' *Anonimo ticinese,*" *Bollettino della Società pavese di storia patria* 1 (1901), 46–57.

tine's bones. The anonymous author was called "Aulico anonimo" (the anonymous courtier or cleric), though some asserted that the author was named Sigisbert. The discovery of a new manuscript, the *Codice Bonetta,* in the middle of the nineteenth century provided new information and the hope that further study might clarify the original purpose of the text and the identity of the author. The significance of the new manuscript had already been noted in the June 27, 1857, *Gazzetta della provincia di Pavia* by Giovanni Bosisio. Luigi de Marchi's article reviewed the different manuscripts of this text and attempted to establish links between them and to determine when the original document had been composed.

Maiocchi and Quintavalle published a new edition of this text in 1903. They reviewed the available manuscripts and, after a thorough consideration, rejected the hypothesis of Luigi de Marchi on the relationship between the different manuscripts. Much of their introduction was spent discussing the personality and identity of the author. They explained the origin of the name Sigisbert as a mistake made by Romualdo Ghisoni in his *Flavia,* and they emphasized the error made by Giuseppe Maria Bellini in accepting Ghisoni's misattribution and Beretti's good sense in questioning it. They described what they believed to be the anonymous author's intellectual, social, and religious background but offered no hypothesis as to his name. A detailed index was included, as well as a chronology prepared by Quintavalle. The edition received a lukewarm review by Romano in the fourth volume of the *Bollettino.*[32] He accepted their refutation of the hypothesis put forth by Luigi de Marchi but regarded the lengthy discussion made about the anonymous author to be no real advance in the knowledge of his identity.

Maiocchi subsequently took on another task—that of editing a new journal in Pavia, the *Rivista di scienze storiche.* At the end of 1905, in the *Bollettino,* Romano noted that an article he had published earlier that year in the *Bollettino* on the curious name of San Pietro in Ciel d'Oro had been treated rather roughly in the October 31 issue of the *Rivista.* He explained that he was not planning a formal response at that time, but we nonetheless see that all was not well between the president and the secretary of the Società. At its January 28, 1906, meeting Maiocchi suddenly resigned as secretary, and from the Società itself, despite an appeal from Giacinto

32. Giacinto Romano, review of *Anonymi ticinensis, Bollettino della Società pavese di storia patria* 4 (1904), 121–27.

Romano that he carry on. A provisional secretary, a G. Marabelli, was appointed for the meeting; a lawyer, Carlo Belli, was elected permanent secretary. The minutes of the meeting do not make clear what prompted Maiocchi's sudden action. One factor that may have been decisive is suggested in the next issue of the *Bollettino:* a devastating review by Romano himself of the first volume of Maiocchi and Nazareno Casacca's *Codex diplomaticus Ord. E. S. Augustini Papiae* (The manuscript documents of the Augustinian Hermits of Pavia).[33] Since it was one of the secretary's duties to edit the *Bollettino,* Maiocchi had probably already seen Romano's review by January 28. Romano's piece was the longest book review that had yet appeared in the *Bollettino.* Romano was, in part, miffed because of the way his 1895 article on the Hermits and Canons had been treated, or rather ignored, in Maiocchi's preface.[34] But the real cause of his anger, and the substance of his review, focused on a couple of specific interpretive points. He accused the editors of a variety of scholarly sins in their transcriptions of the documents. The heart of his criticism was that their work was a slander against the Canons Regular in the guise of a scholarly edition of documents. Because of the prejudices of the editors, he concluded that their work was "deprived of any scientific worth, there being so many errors of fact, of method, of critical judgment, and of reasoning; from the first to the last page the authors give evidence of their complete lack of taste and learning."[35]

A year later, at the meeting of January 20, 1907, Giacinto Romano delivered a speech, which was subsequently published, that in large measure gave his version of the falling-out between himself and Maiocchi. There were, in fact, no hard feelings, according to him; indeed, the resignation was not precipitous at all, for Maiocchi's interests had gradually been

33. Giacinto Romano, "Il codice diplomatico agostiniano di S. Pietro in Ciel d'Oro," *Bollettino della Società pavese di storia patria* 6 (1906), 287–318; see 168–69 for the minutes of the meeting. It is interesting to note that three hundred copies of the *Codex* were printed; this is the same number of copies that had been printed of Beretti's *Lynchnus.*

34. Romano had interpreted the conflict between them as related to the quarrel between the Guelphs, the party of the papacy, and the Ghibellines, the party of the empire. As a supporter of the new, secular Italy, he found that his sympathies lay with the empire. It is in character that the *Festschrift* prepared for Romano and published in Pavia in 1907, *Raccolta di scritti storici in onore del Prof. Giacinto Romano,* contains an early article by Ettore Rotta, "Il Giansenismo in Lombardia e i prodromi del Risorgimento italiano."

35. Romano, "Il codice diplomatico agostiniano," 318.

shifting because of his commitments to the *Rivista*. In his view, in the end, their separation was amicable and would not harm the interests of the Società; their quarrel had been held within proper bounds ("tenuta ne'limiti della correttezza scientifica").[36] The controversy between Romano and Maiocchi continued in the *Bollettino* and the *Rivista*, but the topics moved beyond matters concerning San Pietro and its monks.[37] Maiocchi continued his work on his edition of the documents of the Augustinian Hermits; no comparable edition for the Canons has ever been published.

Cleonice Baggini presented the last scholarly study on the issue of the authenticity of the bones found in San Pietro in Ciel d'Oro as a doctoral dissertation in 1913. The work, less than one hundred typed pages, is titled "Storia della polemica intorno all'identità delle ossa di S. Agostino, vescovo e dottore della chiesa, scoperte l'anno 1695 nella Basilica di S. Pietro in Ciel d'Oro di Pavia" (A history of the controversy concerning the identity of the bones of St. Augustine, bishop and doctor of the Church, discovered in 1695 in the Basilica of San Pietro in Ciel d'Oro, Pavia). Baggini, who was from Pavia, firmly endorsed the conclusions of 1728. His comments on his personal acceptance of the authenticity of the relics from his youth onward echo something of the perspective of Colli. We do not know anything about his reasons for choosing this topic. At this time Maiocchi was completing the last volume of his edition of the documents concerning the Hermits of San Pietro. He may have found the subject to be of interest as well as of practical use to him as he worked his way through the eighteenth century. Perhaps the authenticity of the relics of Augustine was still a matter of speculation and even of humor among the graduate students. Muratori was a favorite among the supporters of the new Italian state, and perhaps the chance to defeat Muratori on his own ground had attractions as well.

Baggini's opening chapter, concerning San Pietro and the various reli-

36. G. Mondaini, "Atti della società," *Bollettino della Società pavese di storia patria* 7 (1907), 3–15, esp. 8.

37. See, for example, Giacinto Romano, "Per un critico innominato," *Bollettino della Società pavese di storia patria* 10 (1910), 506: "The inferior level of the educational and cultural training of the Italian clergy has been lamented many times. It is extremely unpleasant to have to confirm that this dismal reality exists here in the person of a priest who writes for a journal published in Pavia."

gious orders that had occupied it, constituted what might be called a biography of the building and of the inhabitants of that space until the time of the Invention. Chapter 2 juxtaposed the arguments of Muratori and Fontanini; here Baggini's aim was to show that all of Muratori's objections could be answered from Fontanini and other sources, including investigations made in the nineteenth century. Baggini was not permitted to see the bones themselves, but he did view the silver casket from the side of the altar, and he studied the marble casket in the Civic Museum with care. In chapter 3 he explained why he believed that the location of the bones had always been known and reviewed all mentions he could find to prove that there was a continuous knowledge of their location. Indeed, he believed he could prove that even the Canons Regular knew all along where the bones were. Thus, in essence, Baggini agreed with Beretti that there really had not been an Invention at all. Just as chapter 3 dealt with Augustine's possible movements within San Pietro, chapter 4 concerned the rumors that the body had been removed from the church. Relying primarily on textual evidence, Baggini attempted to discredit stories such as those of Basil and Florentius. No mention was made of any discoveries in the recent reconstruction of San Pietro; presumably no new physical evidence had turned up. Baggini was the first to respond to Muratori and to answer his arguments on their own terms. His conclusion was that the bones could be proved by historical argument to be those of St. Augustine.

Baggini does not indicate which members of the faculty evaluated his thesis or who was the primary adviser for his dissertation. Some indications may be gathered from his bibliography, however. Although he lists several books by Maiocchi, not one of Giacinto Romano's is included—though, to be sure, in the text itself there are several positive citations of Romano's scholarly work. The presences and absences in his footnotes and bibliography reflect the politics of his time and the power of the older controversy—the controversy he himself was attempting to put to rest. Baggini's project would have been regarded as an antiquarian investigation with a pro-clerical ax to grind, even if his conclusions were substantially correct.

Like much of the eighteenth-century controversy, Baggini's investigation took place without regard to Augustine's works and the scholarship about it. Interesting things were going on in the world of Augustine scholarship. In 1888, in the *Revue des deux mondes,* Gaston Boissier published an article that questioned the accuracy of Augustine's conversion story. Based on a close reading of what Augustine wrote at Cassiciacum in 386 right after his conversion, his study concluded that the account presented in *The Confessions* was a creative reworking of the event. At the same time, Adolf von Harnack had come to a similar conclusion as to the amount of creative imagination Augustine had used in his attempt to write his own legend.[38] These works mark the beginning of modern *Confessions* criticism. In 1918, Prosper Alfaric radicalized the controversy, concluding that Augustine had been converted in 386, all right, but his conversion was to Neoplatonism. Only later would Augustine rework his story into the edifying masterpiece of rhetoric we find in *The Confessions.* This new critique of how Augustine had created, Catholicized, whitewashed, and retold his own story fitted a pattern of interest expressed by a variety of late-nineteenth- and early-twentieth-century scholars in the origins and meaning of founding myths. There was an expectation that such stories were embedded in the beliefs and practices of many different cultures, peoples, and institutions. The aim of such investigations was not to discredit, rebuke, or ridicule religious sentiment but to understand how such diverse reactions to the experience of the divine might come about and to explore the particular culture that gave that experience life. The results of these investigations have become the scholarly study of myth and the history of religion.

A sign of the times was the creation in Pavia of a new academic journal, *Athenaeum: studi periodici di letteratura e storia* (A periodical for the study of literature and history). Its first issue appeared in January 1913, the same year as Baggini's thesis. In the statement of its mission the journal proclaimed, "The academic fields to which we will give preference will be those concerning mythology, cultural and intellectual history, the history of religion, and classical, medieval, and humanistic literatures."[39] The journal's first issues published reviews of Harnack's work, the Bollandist Hippolite Delehaye's studies on martyrs, and articles by Father Ernesto Buonaiuti, who taught religious history at Rome. It also reviewed the early published works of Raffaele Pettazzoni, who likewise taught at Rome. Pettazzoni relied on the findings of anthropology for his work on the

38. Bradley E. Starr, "Harnack, Adolf von," in *Augustine through the Ages: An Encyclopedia,* ed. Allan D. Fitzgerald (Grand Rapids, Mich.: Eerdmans Publishing, 1999), 414–16.

39. *Athenaeum: studi periodici di letteratura e storia* 1 (1913), 1. The contributions of the journal to these fields were thought to be of such importance that a reprint of the journal was published in 1966.

history of myth and religion. This fortuitous juxtaposition of the journal and the thesis invites the reflection that at this juncture, new methods of scholarship were developing that were appropriate for such subject matter and that could interpret the experience and significance of patron saints in their communities.

The doctoral research of Baggini and the project of the *Athenaeum* developed alongside the cultural and spiritual community that participated in the restoration of Augustine's relics to their traditional place in San Pietro. The affinities that linked these varied interests to Augustine were as nuanced and as deep as those that existed for the workmen who found the bones, the men and women who experienced miraculous cures, as well as those of authors such as Colli, Bellini, and Beretti. From the fourteenth century until the 1780s, an unusual institutional framework had created a situation that prevented there being any official position on Augustine's relics, and this was supported by the conflict between the two Augustinian brotherhoods. Some substantive aspect of the tradition of Augustine and the Augustinians in San Pietro continued after the legislation of enlightened despotism destroyed this peculiar religious community. At the end of the nineteenth century, this traditional feeling, supplemented with substantial financial investment, resulted in the restoration of San Pietro and the most recent Translation of the relics of Augustine.

There is a novel and entertaining aspect to a case like the one concerning the arguments over the authenticity of the relics claimed to be those of St. Augustine. And it is salutary to be reminded of intellectual debates in the early modern period that involved participants from both dominant and subordinate groups of intellectuals, in which the imposition of brutal punishment was absent. There were a few instances of oppression and attempts at compulsion; and there were corresponding moments of resistance. The Pavian participants in the controversy provide some clues as to what had constituted the oral tradition about Augustine and his orders in Pavia. Until the controversy, most saw the division of San Pietro as older than Noah, that is, as going back to the time when the relics first arrived in Pavia. Various authors in the controversy corrected some of these misconceptions: they restored the role of the Benedictines and the edict of John XXII, for example. But we cannot say how this new information affected the oral tradition. In one of its scenes, which was visible for all to see, the *arca* showed that it was the Hermits who had carried Augustine's relics into Pavia. A similar image had been used in the Milan broadside of 1728. We do not know the extent to which the traditional account was influenced or informed by the controversy. Because the controversy concerned an important patron saint, this patchy tradition acquired a more historical character, at least for a while.

Our most direct testimony on the views of illiterate or marginally literate Pavians about St. Augustine's relics confirms their faith in the relics' power but does not tell us about their interpretation or the level of their interest in the issues that were so important to the authors who argued about the authenticity of the bones. We know that some of these semiliterate construction workers had absorbed enough to affirm that the lettering that they had seen was Gothic. Given their acquisition of information about styles of lettering, it is easy to imagine that during the periods of the printed controversy, anyone who was interested could have found someone to bring him up to date on the latest arguments. We do know that some enthusiasm was shown for worshipping the relics that were recovered. Supporters of the Canons criticized the laxity of allowing unsanctioned worship of unauthenticated relics; others suggested that it was pigheaded not to authenticate relics of such clear provenance. A solution to the fundamental issue was determined in 1728; this apparently had a good deal of local support. Nevertheless, when Muratori sought to prove that the correct story of the relics had not yet been written, some in Pavia cared enough to make a manuscript copy of his essay. Signs of resistance to the 1728 decision can be inferred from the fact that publishers seldom produced especially dangerous books without the expectation of purchasers, or at least of some other recompense for their risk. But from the evidence we can glean from the publishing history of the essay, the expected audience was not a Pavian readership. The subsequent history of the relics at Pavia indicates a satisfaction with the assertion of the bones' authenticity; not only did this belief reflect an appreciation for the city's tradition, but also the claim was confirmed by the historical investigations of reputable scholars and the anatomical examination carried out by the university's scientists. Inferences can be drawn about the ways in which readers influenced the arguments of the controversy, but it remains difficult to say how the controversy affected the popular tradition. The appearances based on existing sources suggest that the oral traditions about Augustine in Pavia conform to the officially authenticated written texts and documents.

These sources of evidence, it must be admitted, reflect the political conservatism of the controversialists themselves. The most intense phase of the quarrel took place against a background that saw the fading of an earlier form of political conservatism and its replacement by two characteristic types of modern political conservatism. The Venetian intervention, which took the form of a book review and the essay by Trevisan, exemplified a pattern of early modern conservatism that asserted its authority and enforced its control by emphasizing the distinction between the values, beliefs, and modes of thinking of the dominant group and those of subordinate groups or classes. Social differentiation was a paramount value for the preservation of the Venetian aristocracy; and it was a value shared by the other privileged bodies that made up the various elites of old regime society. There was a natural hierarchy in the state: each status had a rank or degree, and each body or group, when properly constituted, did not challenge its superior; each managed its proper function by following local traditions and practices. Conflict over fundamental issues within the state and within groups themselves, though common, was not natural. Controlled absences of harmony were acceptable and even to be encouraged because they were structured around the return to proper order; rebellion, by contrast, was chaos and the product of a trick or deceit.

The Venetian journalists saw the controversy over the bones as in essence a political quarrel between rival religious orders that were interested in ensuring their power and status, not harmony and justice. Each order in San Pietro had a bee in its bonnet; and this irrational element even affected controversialists from outside Pavia, for they too had used the quarrel to further the interests of their own religious orders. The role of the Venetian journalists was to unmask the pretenses that had prolonged the quarrel, and they presented their own solution. Their authority, they believed, should silence the quarrel. If it continued, their fear was that the papacy would intervene and turn the intellectual hierarchy of Italy topsy-turvy. Their conception of a just, well-ordered, aristocratic Republic of Letters was a moderate form of the aggressive, aristocratic political conservatism that had flourished from the mid-fifteenth century to the crisis years of the mid-seventeenth century. It had been driven by a desire to make ever more rigid the separation of the aristocracy from the unprivileged majority; but this stratification enhanced the anxiety the aristocracy felt about the possible rebellion of its subordinates. This fear nourished the conviction that threats from below could be overawed and thus nipped in the bud by an ostentatious display of vitality that could crush and pacify a potential rival. This heroic attitude had been replaced by a more moderate conception by the early eighteenth century.

In the second phase of the controversy over Augustine's relics, more modern forms of political conservatism dominated the scene. The approaches of Benedict XIII and his supporters, and that of Muratori, exemplify two forms of this modern conservatism. Both continued aspects of the aristocratic conservatism of the Venetians but added other elements distinctive to the development of modern conservatism. Benedict's group saw themselves as upholders of the Catholic tradition; but this did not mean that all of the traditions accepted by any group of Catholics were to be promoted. Rome, its bureaucracy, and its intellectuals and historians identified and confirmed the content of the correct tradition. The task of disciplining and enforcing religious solidarity was as important as it had always been, but the nervous concern over the rebellious masses gave way to a different model of control. Benedict developed an insight of some of his predecessors, who had seen Rome as the protector and the source of legitimacy not only for elite organizations such as religious orders and confraternities, but also for popular devotions and the cult of the saints. Instead of emphasizing distinctions of rank and status, the papacy sought ways to make its authority appear to be an actual presence on the local scene.[40] The pope and his representatives were thus able to work with the traditional conservatism of the urban and rural working poor. This had the practical effect of increasing the image of the papacy as a paternal presence in the life of each parish; Rome's authority was represented as originating not from a remote power center but from an exacting father figure.

Benedict XIII's intervention in Pavia in 1728 was an example of this approach. The strategy of entering into local communities as a patriarchal figure and appealing directly for the loyalty of the faithful entailed enormous risks, however. The reaction to its growing success on the local scene in countries with Catholic sovereigns resulted in a bitter reaction such as we saw in Pavia with the religious reforms of Joseph II. But the loyalty of the parishioners outlasted and in large measure eventually overcame the

40. Margaret Lavinia Anderson, "The Divisions of the Pope: The Catholic Revival and Europe's Transition to Democracy," in *The Politics of Religion: Studies in Nineteenth-Century Europe and Latin America*, ed. Austen Ivereigh (London: Institute of Latin American Studies, 2000), 22–42. She describes the different paths of political Catholicism in the nineteenth century.

reforms planned by the monarchs of the *ancien régime,* as well as the social and political forces set in motion by the French Revolution. Later, conservative leaders, political movements, and parties discovered similar ways of linking their agendas to the traditionalism of both town and country. The practical consequence for Pavia was Benedict's approval of the identification of the bones as being those of St. Augustine, thus ending a contentious issue at San Pietro.

One element of the papacy's institutional conservatism that aided its long-term survival was that it successfully avoided linking its spiritual and interpretive authority to any single theoretical approach or school of theological investigation. By regarding any speculative system, no matter how firmly founded in tradition, as provisional or hypothetical, the papacy preserved itself, much of its tradition, and the institutional forms of the Catholic Church. The refusal to favor the extreme positions on grace, human works, and God's foreknowledge promoted by the Jansenists and the Jesuits was a success. A mistake had been made, it was tacitly admitted, when parts of the papal administration had forbidden the teaching of the Copernican system and condemned Galileo's *Dialogue on the Two Chief World Systems.* The hypothetical method had its uses here: by adding some "supposeds," primarily in the marginal notes, a virtually unchanged edition of Galileo's text was published in Rome in 1741 with papal approval.

The Roman bureaucracy in the eighteenth century followed two distinct impulses. One was a sincere and effective desire to improve, become involved with, and deepen the spiritual life of the individual parish. While the papacy sought to become closer to the people, certain elements within the papal administration separated themselves from the intellectual community of Italy. They condemned the writings of Giannone, Montesquieu, and Beccaria for advocating a separation of church and state and declaring that the Roman Church should leave politics to secular rulers. Those in the Church hierarchy who shaped this policy cut themselves off from the actual intellectual life experienced by most clerical and secular intellectuals in Italy and the European Catholic community.

Muratori's conservatism distrusted reforms planned on the basis of abstract principles, but he was sympathetic to reforms undertaken by secular rulers. His preference was for solving practical, narrowly defined problems with limited, flexible solutions. While he granted that the maze of law courts and their badly defined jurisdictions made the legal procedures of Lombardy a disaster, he still looked askance at the prospect that administrators in Vienna might draft a uniform law code. His preference was to single out certain problems and publicize specific inequities or abuses to ensure that the unwary would not be entrapped in them. Laws should be changed only as a final measure, he believed, and then in a piecemeal fashion. Typical of his pragmatic approach was his attitude toward the charging of interest, which had been forbidden, at least in certain forms, by Church law. He could see no harm in charging interest—certainly not what he viewed as a moderate rate, a couple of percent. Moderate interest made business possible, and Christ could not have been opposed to that, he argued. But Muratori was opposed to what he considered excessive or usurious interest rates, though this too admitted of variation based on specific local circumstance. He differed with the papal administrators, though, on the issue of who had the best view of local circumstance; here Muratori tended to support the perspective of the local secular traditions. On the bones found in Pavia, he believed that the clear historical tradition suggested that Augustine's relics had been well hidden. To identify remains found so close to the surface as being those of Augustine showed disrespect to the most authentic memories about these relics. The least violence to the evidence would have been caused by reaffirming Augustine's presence in San Pietro but ruling that the precise location had not yet been found.

His conservatism had some significant differences from the position of Rome. Muratori accepted the truth of the Catholic religion and its evident superiority over all other faiths. Its truths could and ought to be investigated and discussed in a rational manner, but he agreed with the orthodox position that the free examination of these matters had always resulted in confusion and contradiction. This showed the basic fallibility of human reason unguided by revelation. The papacy, in his view, had certain clear responsibilities in matters of religious doctrine and practice. And Muratori accepted its wisdom in not accepting any one method or theoretical system as authoritative. His study of historical documents had persuaded him that human affairs were local matters whose administration was best carried out by individuals who used their common sense and practical reason to achieve what seemed the most desirable result. And with many of his age, he identified this common sense as a mean between a corrosive skepticism that doubted and mocked everything and a casuistry that pardoned and permitted everything. His resolution of these epistemological and ethical dilemmas was supplemented and refined by his study of human history and its documents. Despite his moderation, he regarded Protestants as heretics and accepted the general damnation of non-Christians. At the same time, he first gained notoriety for his resolute defense of a secular ruler against the legal claims of the papacy over the Comacchio region.

Muratori, like the Venetians, had no interest in appealing to a popular audience, though he was committed to communicating his knowledge to the public, by which he meant the educated general reader. But the kind of pretentious unmasking exemplified by the Venetian journalists failed, in his view, to address the fundamental issues of religious history. Ascribing or identifying low motives to religious leaders or institutions reduced ecclesiastical history to the terms of political history alone. Such an approach failed to address the spiritual values, however confusedly understood, that shaped the historical and cultural life of the Christian centuries. The Venetian method might provide the politics of religion, but it had no respect for the religious phenomenon itself. Muratori's conception of the range of genuine religious life was limited to the Christian/Catholic experience. Within that limitation, he recognized that the unlearned could make contributions that were not mental delusions. This did not mean that popular traditions were immune from unfortunate influences. Manifestations of the religious impulse deserved deep respect in accord with the sanctity and humanity of each individual believer. This, in turn, led him to criticize aspects of the political regimes of his day. An observation that repeats itself more frequently as Muratori brought the *Annals* of Italian history up to his own time is that poor Italians living in towns and the countryside had suffered, and continued to suffer, too much from the waste of war. Something was wrong with politics and with the leaders who could abuse their people over and over.

Muratori's conservatism differed from that of the papacy in his respect for the inner illumination of the believer and the inspiration of the scholarly mind which resolutely seeks the truth. He was not very concerned with the outer forms of religious life. More important to him was an inner freedom or liberty, which in Muratori's belief guided the Catholic scholar in accord with true piety and religion. Muratori may be described as a Catholic version of the "pietistic" conservative, identified by Karl Mannheim in *Ideology and Utopia*[41] as one of the major types of the conservative

41. Karl Mannheim, *Ideology and Utopia: An Introduction to the Sociology of Knowledge,* trans. Louis Wirth and Edward Shils (New York: Harcourt, Brace and World, 1968), 238–39.

utopian mentality. Muratori's reliance on the inner subjectivity of the historical researcher to articulate and interpret the complex inheritance of a people and their region contrasts with the more realistic conservatism represented by the papacy of Benedict. Curiously, we might find Benedict's commitment to local religious practice of more interest than the private, intellectual spirituality of Muratori. Benedict believed that symbolic rituals facilitated the spontaneous, willed acceptance of a value or belief by both rulers and ruled and that it could create consensus outside the usual determinants of force and control. One of the accomplishments of the modern study of the history of religions and of its symbolism is that such phenomena can be profitably studied as religious phenomena, and not only as an aspect of political manipulation and ideology.

In Pavia, the local habits of discourse and print culture interacted with older forms of the city's involvement with its religious tradition. The adherents of these three cosmopolitan conservative positions found little to engage them in the temporary readers of Pavia, though each group justified their involvement in the quarrel because of their interest in authentic local traditions. Communities of book readers and of storytellers were of marginal concern. The story of the identification of Augustine's bones is one of the many unanticipated consequences of Augustine's life, his books, and his influence. Printed material about the issue interacted with the marginally literate and with other general readers. We can recognize something of their excitement, anticipation, and uncertainty and speculate on the momentary impact of their reading and listening. Finally, authors, teachers, librarians, and others who work in the book trade, all adjusting to a new world in which information can be visited and downloaded by any reader without the use of a book or special training, may find this account of an earlier community of temporary readers who sought information from print salutary and encouraging.

INDEX

Harold Samuel Stone was born in Washington, D.C. He was educated at St. John's College and the University of Chicago, where he received his Ph.D. from the Committee on Social Thought. He has taught at Northwestern University, Colgate University, and American University in Cairo and is currently on the faculty of Shimer College in Illinois. He has been awarded several grants and fellowships, including a Gladys Krieble Delmas Foundation Fellowship and a National Endowment for the Humanities Summer Seminar stipend. Professor Stone is the author of *Vico's Cultural History: The Production and Transmission of Ideas in Naples, 1685–1750* (1997) and numerous articles on the intellectual history of early modern Europe. He is coeditor of Montesquieu's *Spirit of the Laws* for Cambridge Texts in the History of Political Thought (1989). He lives in Waukegan, Illinois, and Cooperstown, New York, with Melissa McAfee, Emily Stone, and Edward Stone. His email address is harold@shimer.edu.